PAT BROWN, MBA

TrackMoney101

Using Track to Teach the Basics of Money

ABRAM 47 BROWN

First published by AbramBrown47 2026

First edition

ISBN: 978-1-967737-60-4

This book was professionally typeset on Reedsy.
Find out more at reedsy.com

Contents

Foreword

Track teaches you a truth most people never fully learn.

There are no shortcuts.

You can have talent. You can have speed. You can have great spikes and a fast start. None of it matters if you do not respect the process. The runner who skips base mileage, rushes workouts, or ignores recovery might look good early in the season, but they rarely finish strong. Eventually, the body gives out. The results fade. The race exposes what preparation tried to hide.

Money works the same way.

This book exists because too many athletes are handed financial responsibility without the training to handle it. Track athletes, in particular, understand discipline, sacrifice, and delayed gratification better than most. You know what it means to train when nobody is watching. You know what it feels like to run alone, lap after lap, chasing a standard that only the clock can measure. And yet, when the uniform comes off, many of those same athletes feel unprepared for money decisions that last far longer than any season.

That disconnect is not your fault.

Athletes are developed inside systems. Schedules are set. Travel is arranged. Meals are planned. Training cycles are structured. The entire environment is designed to help you perform. Financial life, on the other hand, often arrives with no coaching, no reps, and no playbook. One day you are focused on splits, recovery, and qualifying marks. The next day you are expected to manage income, expenses, debt, investing, insurance, and long-term planning on your own.

That transition is jarring.

What Track Money 101 recognizes is that athletes already have the mindset needed to succeed financially. What they lack is translation. Track teaches pacing. Money requires pacing. Track rewards consistency. Money compounds through consistency. Track punishes impatience. Money does too. The skills are transferable once you see the connection.

This book is not about chasing fast money or flashy results. It is about running your own race with discipline and intention. It is about learning when to push, when to hold back, and when to trust the training you have put in. Just like track, financial success is built over time, not in one meet or one moment.

You will not find hype here.

You will find fundamentals.

You will find reminders that matter when the race gets uncomfortable. You will find systems that help you stay on pace when others sprint too early. And you will find reassurance that you do not need to be perfect to finish strong. You just need to stay disciplined and keep moving forward.

Track athletes understand something most people forget. Winning is rarely about the first 100 meters. It is about who still has form, strength, and focus when the race demands it most. Money is no different. Early success does not guarantee a strong finish. Preparation does.

This book is your training plan for money. Not a guarantee. Not a shortcut. A system. If you respect it the same way you respected your training, it can help you avoid the mistakes that derail too many talented people after competition ends.

Run your race.

Trust the process.

Finish strong.

Introduction

Every track athlete learns this lesson early, whether they want to or not.

You cannot fake fitness.

You can cut a workout short. You can skip mileage. You can convince yourself that talent will cover the gap. For a while, it might. You might still hit a decent time. You might even win a race. But eventually, the finish line tells the truth. The athlete who tried to cheat the process fades. The athlete who respected the work keeps moving.

Money exposes people the same way the track does.

From the outside, financial success often looks sudden. Someone buys a house. Someone invests early. Someone seems "ahead." What you do not see is the years of preparation behind it or, just as often, the stress, debt, and fragility hidden underneath the surface. Just like racing, outcomes do not tell the whole story. The process does.

This book starts with one core idea: there are no shortcuts to the finish line with money.

That does not mean money has to be complicated. It means it has to be intentional.

Track athletes understand pacing better than most people. You know the danger of going out too fast. You know the panic that sets in when the lactic acid hits early. You know how painful it feels to realize you burned too much energy before the race really began. Financial life has the same traps. Overspending early. Taking on too much debt. Chasing fast returns. Ignoring recovery and protection. The consequences may not show up immediately, but they show up eventually.

Many athletes struggle financially not because they lack discipline, but because they apply discipline in the wrong places. They train relentlessly, but freestyle their money. They respect a training plan, but react emotionally to financial decisions. They understand long-term development in sport, but expect instant results with money.

That mismatch creates frustration.

Money feels overwhelming because it does not come with a coach yelling splits. There is no scoreboard lighting up in real time. There is no meet schedule forcing accountability. Instead, there are quiet decisions. Automatic spending. Delayed consequences. Long timelines. That environment punishes impatience and rewards consistency, even though it rarely feels that way in the moment.

Track athletes already have the tools to win financially. You know how to delay gratification. You know how to trust boring work. You know how to show up when nobody is watching. You know that confidence comes from preparation, not from hype. What you may not have is a way to connect those instincts to money decisions.

That is what this book is designed to do.

Track Money 101 does not promise fast results. It does not offer hacks. It does not pretend that one smart decision fixes everything. Instead, it treats money the way track treats performance: as a long-term process built on fundamentals, repetition, and awareness.

You will see familiar themes throughout this book. Base training matters. Recovery matters. Protection matters. Efficiency matters. Timing matters. You will see why sprinting too early financially can be just as damaging as sprinting too early in a race. You will learn how to build systems that help you stay on pace when emotions and outside pressure try to pull you off plan.

Most importantly, this book reframes success.

In track, winning is not always about the podium. Sometimes it is about running your best race. Sometimes it is about staying healthy. Sometimes it is about improving year over year. Financial success works the same way. It is not about comparing yourself to someone else's highlight. It is about building a life that holds together under pressure and still moves forward when conditions change.

There will be moments in your financial life that feel like the final lap. Fatigue sets in. Distractions get loud. The temptation to make a desperate move shows up. This book is meant to prepare you for those moments before they happen. Not with fear, but with clarity.

You do not need to be perfect with money.

You do need to be consistent.

You do not need to win every race.

You do need to finish strong.

Track teaches that the race is honest. Money is honest too. It rewards patience. It punishes shortcuts. It reflects habits over time, not intentions in the moment.

As you move through this book, treat it the way you treated training. Learn the fundamentals. Respect the process. Trust that small, disciplined decisions stack up. If you do that, you do not need shortcuts.

You already know how to finish a race.

Now it is time to learn how to finish the financial one just as strong.

About This Book

Track and field is one of the most honest sports there is.

There are no teammates to hide behind. No clock to manage strategically. No referee calls to blame. The race gives you exactly what you earned in training, nothing more and nothing less. You cannot shortcut conditioning. You cannot fake endurance. You cannot borrow fitness from someone else. The stopwatch tells the truth every time.

Money works the same way.

This book is built on the belief that track athletes already understand the most important principles of financial success, even if no one has ever connected the dots for them. Pacing. Discipline. Repetition. Recovery. Patience. Awareness. These are not just athletic concepts. They are life skills. When applied to money, they determine whether you build something sustainable or burn out early.

Track Money 101 is not a traditional personal finance book. It does not talk down to you. It does not assume you are careless, reckless, or incapable. It assumes the opposite. It assumes you know how to work. It assumes you know how to suffer. It assumes you know that results come from process, not promises.

What most athletes never receive is translation.

In track, you are taught exactly how to prepare for competition. Training cycles are planned months in advance. Mileage is built gradually. Intensity is added carefully. Rest is scheduled intentionally. You trust the plan because you have seen what happens when you abandon it. Money, on the other hand, is usually left to improvisation. You earn it without guidance. You spend it without structure. You invest it based on noise. Then you are surprised when things feel out of control.

This book exists to close that gap.

Every chapter uses track and field as the primary language for explaining financial decisions. Not because analogies are cute, but because they are effective. You already understand what happens when you go out too fast. You already understand overtraining. You already understand false starts, poor pacing, missed recovery, and trying to peak too early. Financial mistakes follow the same patterns.

When this book talks about budgeting, it treats it like base mileage. When it talks about saving, it treats it like daily training. When it talks about investing, it treats it like race execution. When it talks about risk, it treats it like pacing strategy. When it talks about protection and insurance, it treats it like staying healthy enough to compete.

Nothing here is theoretical.

Just as track careers are shaped by habits built when nobody is watching, financial outcomes are shaped by small decisions made consistently over time. This book is designed to help you recognize those moments and respond to them with the same discipline you brought to training.

Another core belief behind this book is that speed is overrated without efficiency.

Many people chase money the way inexperienced runners chase fast times. They sprint early. They ignore form. They skip recovery. They assume effort alone will carry them. Sometimes it works briefly. More often, it leads to burnout, injury, or regret. Track Money 101 emphasizes efficiency over excitement. It teaches you how to keep moving forward without wasting energy or creating unnecessary risk.

This book also respects the reality that athletes are not all the same.

Sprinters, middle-distance runners, distance runners, jumpers, throwers, and multi-event athletes all approach training differently. Money works the same way. Your background, income, career path, and life responsibilities matter. There is no single "right" financial strategy, just like there is no single training plan that works for every athlete. The goal is not to copy someone else's race. The goal is to run yours well.

Throughout the book, you will see an emphasis on long-term thinking.

Track teaches you to think in seasons, not single races. You build toward peaks. You accept setbacks. You adjust when things do not go as planned. Financial life requires the same mindset. One bad year does not define you. One good year does not mean the work is done. What matters is staying healthy, staying disciplined, and staying in the race long enough for progress to compound.

You will also notice what this book does not do.

It does not promise shortcuts.

It does not glorify risk.

It does not encourage speculation.

It does not shame mistakes.

Mistakes are part of development. What matters is learning from them before they compound into something harder to fix. Track athletes understand this instinctively. You review the race. You adjust training. You come back better prepared.

That is the rhythm this book follows.

Each chapter is meant to feel like a coaching conversation, not a lecture. Direct. Practical. Grounded in reality. The tone assumes you have been coached hard before and respect structure. It speaks to you the way a good coach would speak about preparation, discipline, and accountability.

At its core, Track Money 101 is about finishing well.

Not just financially, but mentally and emotionally. Money should support your life, not dominate it. It should give you options, not anxiety. It should allow you to stay focused on what matters, not constantly worry about what might go wrong.

Track teaches that races are won by athletes who respect the process from day one. Money rewards the same behavior.

If you are willing to train your financial habits the way you trained your body, this book will feel familiar. You already know how to show up. You already know how to be patient. You already know how to trust boring work.

This book simply gives you a playbook to apply those instincts beyond the track.

The finish line is not a moment. It is a direction.
This book is here to help you stay on it.

Foolish Assumptions

Every good coach starts with assumptions.

Not excuses. Not hype. Assumptions.

They assume you can work. They assume you can learn. They assume you can handle honesty. They assume you are capable of more than you think, even if you are not there yet. Those assumptions shape how you are coached, how you are challenged, and how much responsibility you are given.

This book makes a few assumptions too. They are "foolish" only in the sense that most of the world does not make them about athletes once the uniform comes off.

Here is what this book assumes about you.

This Book Assumes You Understand Discipline

You know what it means to show up when you do not feel like it.

You have trained early in the morning, late at night, in bad weather, and when motivation was gone. You understand that results do not come from intensity alone. They come from consistency. From reps. From doing the work even when nobody is watching.

This book assumes you are capable of building financial discipline because you have already done it physically.

You may not have been taught how to apply that discipline to money, but the muscle already exists.

This Book Assumes You Respect Fundamentals

Track does not reward shortcuts.

If your form is off, it shows.

If your pacing is wrong, it shows.

If you skip base training, it shows.

This book assumes you understand that fundamentals matter more than flash. That boring work compounds. That skipping steps eventually costs you more than it saves.

Financial fundamentals work the same way. Budgeting. Saving. Managing risk. Staying consistent. None of it is glamorous. All of it matters.

This book assumes you are willing to master basics before chasing difficulty.

This Book Assumes You Have Been Misinformed, Not Lazy

If money feels confusing, overwhelming, or frustrating, this book does not assume it is because you are careless or irresponsible.

It assumes you were never given a system.

You were coached in your sport. You were not coached in money.

You were given training plans. You were not given financial playbooks.

You were held accountable for performance. You were rarely taught how to measure financial progress.

Confusion is a predictable outcome of missing structure, not a personal failure.

This book assumes you want to do better once you understand how.

This Book Assumes You Are Not Looking for Shortcuts

Track teaches a hard truth early.

There is no hack for conditioning.

There is no trick for endurance.

There is no substitute for preparation.

This book assumes you already know that anything promising "easy money" should be questioned immediately. You have seen what happens when athletes try to skip steps or peak too early. You have lived the consequences of poor pacing.

This book assumes you are here to build something sustainable, not chase hype.

This Book Assumes You Can Handle Accountability

Coaches do not sugarcoat feedback because clarity matters more than comfort.

This book operates the same way.

It assumes you can look honestly at your habits.

It assumes you can accept responsibility without shame.

It assumes you can separate who you are from what you need to improve.

Money mistakes are not character flaws. They are feedback. Ignoring them makes things worse. Facing them makes progress possible.

This book assumes you are capable of honest self-assessment.

This Book Assumes You Care About the Long Game

Track careers are short. Life is not.

This book assumes you are thinking beyond the next paycheck, the next season, or the next opportunity. It assumes you care about how today's decisions affect your options five, ten, or twenty years from now.

You understand that one race does not define a career.

One good year does not define a life.

One mistake does not end the story.

This book assumes you are willing to trade short-term comfort for long-term control.

This Book Assumes You Are Still an Athlete, Even If You No Longer Compete

Being an athlete is not just something you were. It is something you learned.

You learned how to prepare.

You learned how to take coaching.

You learned how to recover from setbacks.

You learned how to pursue improvement without guarantees.

Those skills did not disappear when competition ended. They simply lost a clear outlet.

This book assumes you can redirect that athlete mindset toward money, career, and life decisions in a way that serves you instead of working against you.

This Book Does Not Assume Perfection

It does not assume you have done everything right.

It does not assume you are starting early.

It does not assume you have avoided mistakes.

It assumes you are willing to learn.

Track athletes know that progress is rarely linear. There are missed races. Injuries. Bad days. Setbacks that require adjustment. Financial progress follows the same pattern.

The goal is not a perfect routine.

The goal is staying upright and finishing strong.

Final Assumption

This book assumes you are capable of more structure than you have been given and more success than you have been shown how to manage.

If that assumption feels uncomfortable, good.

Growth usually does.

This book is written for athletes who are ready to stop improvising with money and start applying the same discipline that once made them competitive.

You already know how to train.

Now you are learning where to apply it.

How This Playbook Is Organized

Track and field is not random.

You do not wake up one day and decide to run a personal best without a plan. Training is layered. Base miles come before speed work. Strength comes before power. Technique comes before execution. Peaking only works if the foundation underneath it is solid.

This book is organized the same way.

It is not designed to be read like a rulebook or a finance textbook. It is built like a training cycle. Each part prepares you for the next. Skip steps, and things feel confusing. Follow the sequence, and the system starts to make sense.

Here is how to use this playbook.

Front Matter: Setting the Mindset

The opening sections are about framing, not tactics.

Before talking about money, you need context. Why money feels harder after track. Why perfectionism shows up. Why discipline without structure breaks down. Why there are no shortcuts that actually last.

Just like a coach sets expectations before the season starts, these sections set the tone. They are meant to reset how you think about money before you try to change behavior.

If you skip this part, you may understand the mechanics later but miss the mindset that makes them stick.

Part I: Base Training and Fundamentals

You cannot race well without a base.

This section covers the fundamentals most athletes were never taught because someone else always handled them. Cash flow. Budgeting. Banking. Credit. Debt. The basics that determine whether you are running smoothly or constantly fighting resistance.

Think of this as aerobic work and form drills.

It is not flashy.

It is not exciting.

It is essential.

If money has ever felt chaotic, this is why. Weak fundamentals make everything else harder. This section is about stability and control so you stop wasting energy.

Part II: Risk Management and Staying Healthy

You do not train hard if you are injured.

This section focuses on protection. Risk awareness. Insurance. Guardrails that keep one bad moment from wiping out months or years of progress.

Track athletes understand this instinctively. You manage workload. You respect recovery. You protect availability.

Money works the same way. You cannot build if one unexpected event knocks you out of the race. This section is about staying healthy financially so you can keep competing long-term.

Part III: Running Efficiently (Investing Fundamentals)

Once the base is built and protection is in place, efficiency matters more than speed.

This section introduces investing, but not in a hype-driven way. Markets. Stocks. Bonds. Funds. Compounding. The systems behind long-term growth.

This is where many athletes rush too early in real life. They want returns before fundamentals. This book does not do that.

Investing here is framed as pacing. Clean mechanics. Consistent effort. Avoiding wasted motion. Efficiency over ego.

Part IV: Race Strategy and Adjustments

Even the best plan requires adjustment.

This section covers asset allocation, buying and holding, rebalancing, and the mental side of money. How to respond when markets move. When life changes. When emotions show up.

In track, you do not panic if the race feels different than expected. You adjust your stride, breathing, and focus without abandoning the plan.

Financially, this is where discipline is tested. This section helps you stay composed instead of reacting.

Part V: The Long Season and Life Beyond Competition

Track careers end. Financial lives do not.

This section zooms out. Taxes. Retirement. Housing. Careers. Family conversations. Estate planning. These are not "later problems." They are long-horizon decisions that shape freedom and stress levels for decades.

Think of this as planning for longevity. Training smart so you are not burned out or broken later.

The focus shifts from performance to sustainability.

Part VI: Finishing Strong

Every race ends. How you finish matters.

The final section addresses advisors, scams, common mistakes, and long-term rules for success. This is about avoiding late-race errors that undo good work.

Just like form matters most when fatigue sets in, financial discipline matters most when pressure increases or opportunity shows up.

How to Read This Book

You can read this book straight through, like a season-long plan.

You can also come back to specific sections when you need them, like revisiting workouts during different phases of training.

What matters most is not speed. It is application.

Read a chapter.

Reflect on it.

Apply one concept.

Then move on.

This playbook is not about knowing more. It is about executing better.

You already know how to train.

This book shows you where to apply that training so you can pace your money, protect your progress, and finish strong.

About Pat Brown

Pat Brown played college football at the University of Kansas from 1994 to 1999 and was named team captain for the 1999 season. His years in the locker room shaped how he thinks about accountability, discipline, preparation, and leadership. Those lessons did not end when football did. They became the foundation for how he approaches work, decision-making, and long-term success.

After his playing career, Pat transitioned into financial services and built a career as a financial advisor and wealth manager. He works with individuals, families, business owners, and athletes who are navigating increasingly complex financial lives. Along the way, he pursued advanced education and professional development, earning an MBA along with industry designations including ChFC®, RICP®, and CAP®. His background blends academic training with real-world experience in financial planning, retirement income strategies, tax planning, and philanthropy.

As the college sports landscape changed with the introduction of Name, Image, and Likeness opportunities, Pat recognized a growing education gap. Student-athletes were gaining access to income, contracts, and endorsements without the financial knowledge required to manage taxes, cash flow, business structures, and long-term consequences. That gap became the catalyst for his work in athlete financial education and the NIL space.

Pat has since become a recognized voice in athlete financial literacy and has been interviewed by national publications and platforms including *Financial Planning*, *Yahoo*, and *ESPN Andscape*. In these conversations, he shares insights on NIL planning, financial literacy gaps, and the challenges facing student-athletes and their families as opportunity arrives faster than education.

These experiences led Pat to author a series of practical, athlete-focused books designed to meet athletes and families where they are. His NIL-related titles include *Financial Literacy for NIL, Financial Literacy for NIL for Parents of Student Athletes, Financial Literacy for NIL for High School Students,* and *Financial Literacy for NIL for International Student Athletes.* Each book is written to be clear, accessible, and grounded in real-world scenarios rather than theory.

Pat also created a growing collection of sport-specific financial education titles, including *Football Money 101, Baseball Money 101, Basketball Money 101, Cheer Money 101, Dance Money 101, Gymnastics Money 101, Hockey Money 101, Lacrosse Money 101, Rowing Money 101, Soccer Money 101, Softball Money 101, Tennis Money 101, Track Money 101, Volleyball Money 101,* and *Wrestling Money 101.* Each book translates the culture, discipline, and mindset of a specific sport into financial lessons athletes can apply long after competition ends.

To extend this mission beyond books, Pat founded **Former Student Athlete**, a platform created to support athletes navigating life after sports. Former Student Athlete provides education, community, and real-world resources focused on financial literacy, career transitions, health, identity, and long-term success once the uniform comes off. You can explore this work at:

- www.formerstudentathlete.com
- www.financialliteracyfornil.com
- www.financialliteracyforstudentathletes.com

Pat is easy to find through a Google search, on LinkedIn, or on Twitter, where he regularly shares insights on athletes, money, and life after sports. If you would like to connect with Pat specifically about *Track Money 101,* you can reach him directly at:

info@trackmoney101.com

Pat's work is rooted in a belief shaped by both football and finance.

Athletes deserve a better playbook for life after sports, and financial education should arrive before opportunity turns into regret.

Part I: Base Training and Fundamentals (Preseason)

You cannot race well without a strong base.

Before speed work, before competition spikes, before race tactics, every successful track season is built on base training. Long runs. Repeated drills. Form checks. Conditioning that feels boring but creates durability. Skip the base and everything else breaks down. You tighten up late in races. You panic under pressure. You fade when it matters.

Money works the same way.

If your financial base is weak, everything feels harder than it should. Bills feel urgent. Decisions feel rushed. Opportunities feel dangerous instead of exciting. You are constantly reacting instead of executing a plan.

This section is your preseason.

It is not flashy.

It is not fast.

It is foundational.

Part I focuses on the financial equivalent of base mileage, form work, and early-season conditioning. These are the skills that keep you steady when life speeds up and pressure shows up.

In Part I, you will learn how to:

- Understand why money feels confusing after track
- Read your financial situation clearly instead of guessing
- Build structure through budgeting and saving

- Manage credit and debt without false starts
- Organize your banking system so nothing leaks

These chapters are about pacing, discipline, and control.

You are not racing yet.

You are building endurance.

When the base is strong, speed becomes sustainable.

When the fundamentals are clean, the finish takes care of itself.

Chapter 1: Why Money Feels Confusing After Track

Every runner remembers the first time a workout went sideways. You showed up confident. Legs felt good. The pace looked manageable on paper. Then halfway through, everything tightened up. Breathing got shallow. Form broke down. Suddenly you were fighting just to finish something you thought you had under control.

It was not because you were weak.

It was because you were running without the right base.

Money feels confusing for former track athletes for the same reason.

Most athletes do not struggle financially because they are careless or irresponsible. They struggle because they are asked to perform in a completely new environment without training, structure, or coaching. One season, your life is organized around practice schedules, training plans, meets, recovery, and accountability. The next, the whistle blows, the season ends, and you are expected to manage income, expenses, credit, taxes, and long-term decisions on your own.

No warm-up.

No walkthrough.

No coach breaking it down.

That is not a failure of effort.

That is a failure of preparation.

Why Financial Literacy Is Rarely Taught to Athletes

Track athletes grow up inside highly structured systems.

Training plans are written for you.

Practice times are fixed.

Travel is handled.

Meals are planned.

Recovery is scheduled.

Your job is to show up, execute, and compete.

That structure is intentional. It allows athletes to focus on performance, not logistics. But it creates a blind spot when the structure disappears.

Financial education often falls into the category of "someone else will handle it."

Schools assume families will teach it.

Families assume athletes will learn later.

Coaches focus on performance, not paychecks.

By the time real money shows up—job income, NIL income, bonuses, sponsorships—the education is already late.

In track terms, this is like entering a championship race without ever learning pacing strategy. You may be talented. You may be fit. But without understanding how to distribute effort, you burn out early or tighten up late.

Money requires pacing.

Nobody teaches athletes how to pace financially.

Money Myths Passed Through Locker Rooms and Training Groups

Every training group has financial noise.

Someone knows a runner who "hit it big" in crypto.

Someone says investing is gambling.

Someone insists saving is pointless if you are young.

Someone claims debt is either evil or harmless.

The loudest voice usually sounds the most confident. Confidence spreads fast, especially in competitive environments. Unfortunately, confidence is not the same as correctness.

Common myths sound like this:

- "If you are not investing aggressively, you are falling behind."
- "Saving is for people who do not make enough."
- "You need multiple income streams right away."
- "Debt is bad no matter what."
- "Debt does not matter if you can make the payments."

These myths feel simple and emotional. That is why they stick.

Track athletes would never overhaul their training based on one random conversation. You would not abandon your program because someone claimed they ran a personal best doing something extreme for a week. Money deserves the same discipline.

Simple advice is not always good advice.

Fast advice is rarely durable advice.

Saving vs Investing vs Gambling

This is one of the most important distinctions in the entire book.

Saving, investing, and gambling are not the same thing, even though people often use them interchangeably.

Saving is about protection.

It is money you can access quickly without risk. Emergency funds. Short-term goals. Stability.

Investing is about ownership and growth over time.

It requires patience. Prices move. Results are uneven. Progress comes from staying in the system, not timing the perfect moment.

Gambling is chasing outcomes without a plan.

No margin for error. No protection. Emotion-driven decisions.

In track terms:

Saving is base mileage and conditioning.

Investing is structured training cycles aimed at long-term performance.

Gambling is sprinting all-out from the gun and hoping you hold on.

Many athletes skip saving because it feels slow. They jump straight to investing or speculation because it feels productive. That is like skipping base training and jumping into speed work year-round. It works briefly. Then injuries, burnout, and inconsistency show up.

Saving protects you.

Investing grows you.

Gambling guesses.

When you confuse these roles, money starts feeling chaotic.

Why Discipline Beats Sprinting Too Early

Track athletes understand one universal truth.

You do not win races in the first 100 meters.

You win by controlling effort, maintaining form, and staying composed while others panic. The athletes who sprint too early may look great for a moment, but they pay for it later.

Money punishes early sprinting the same way.

Spending everything you earn because income feels good.

Taking on debt because payments seem manageable.

Chasing high returns because patience feels boring.

These are financial versions of going out too fast.

Discipline does not feel exciting.

Discipline feels controlled.

The athletes who succeed financially are not the ones chasing perfect scores or fast wins. They are the ones who respect the process, build a base, and stay consistent when progress feels slow.

Money rewards endurance, not bursts.

The Gap Between Training and Real Life

One reason money feels overwhelming is because track provides constant feedback.

Times. Splits. Rankings. Results.

You always know where you stand.

Money feedback is quieter.

Small purchases do not hurt immediately.

Missed savings does not sting right away.

Debt feels fine until flexibility disappears.

The consequences show up later, when adjustment is harder.

That delay creates confusion. Athletes are used to immediate cause and effect. Money operates on lag. What you do today often shows up years later.

Understanding that lag is critical.

Financial discipline today is training for a race you have not run yet.

Coach's Perspective

If a track coach were talking about money, the message would sound familiar.

"Respect the process."

"Do not sprint the first lap."

"Stick to the plan."

"Reps matter."

"Discipline equals freedom."

Coaches do not design training to feel good in the moment. They design it to work over time. Money requires the same mindset.

You do not need to be perfect.

You need to be consistent.

Game Situations and Decision Points

Situation 1: You receive your first real paycheck.

Do you spend freely because you earned it, or do you protect part of it immediately?

Situation 2: You hear about an aggressive investment opportunity.

Do you jump in because you do not want to miss out, or do you ask where it fits in your plan?

Situation 3: You realize you have no emergency savings.

Do you ignore it and hope nothing happens, or start building protection now?

These are pacing decisions.

The wrong choice does not always hurt immediately.

It hurts when the race gets long.

Common Athlete Mistakes and Financial Parallels

Track athletes sometimes go out too fast.

Financially, that looks like overspending early income.

Track athletes sometimes chase workouts instead of consistency.

Financially, that looks like chasing hot investments.

Track athletes sometimes skip base training because it feels boring.

Financially, that looks like skipping saving.

The same behaviors that lose races create financial stress.

Winning the Long Game

Track careers are short. Financial lives are long.

You do not need to win today.

You need to stay in the race.

Money becomes less confusing when you stop trying to sprint through it. When you treat finances like training—structured, paced, repetitive—clarity replaces stress.

Perfect scores do not matter if you cannot finish.
Fast starts do not matter if you fade.
Discipline beats sprinting too early.

Athlete Takeaways

- Build your financial base before chasing speed
- Saving protects you, investing grows you, gambling guesses
- Ignore locker room myths and trust the process
- Discipline and pacing win long races
- Stay consistent and finish strong

Chapter 2: Check Your Starting Blocks: Your Financial Snapshot

Every track athlete knows the feeling of stepping into the blocks. Before the gun goes off, nothing else matters. Not the crowd. Not the competition. Not how hard training has been. The only thing that matters is your position. Feet set. Hands placed. Hips steady. If your setup is off, the race is compromised before it even starts.

Money works the same way.

Before you try to improve anything financially—before investing, saving aggressively, or making big decisions—you have to know where you are starting. Not where you think you are. Not where you hope you are. Where you actually are.

That is your financial snapshot.

Most former athletes avoid this step. Not because they are irresponsible, but because no one taught them how to read the numbers. Money feels scattered. Accounts are spread out. Bills hit at different times. Spending happens automatically. Instead of checking the data, people rely on gut feel.

That is how small problems quietly grow.

Before you adjust pace, you check the blocks.

Income, Expenses, and Cash Flow

Cash flow is how money moves through your life.

Income is what comes in.

Paychecks. Bonuses. Side work. NIL income. Performance incentives.

Expenses are what go out.

Rent. Utilities. Food. Transportation. Subscriptions. Lifestyle spending.

Cash flow is the difference between the two.

In track terms, income is effort output. Expenses are energy drain. Cash flow tells you whether you are sustaining pace or fading.

Many athletes focus only on income. More money feels like progress. But if spending rises at the same rate, nothing actually improves. A higher paycheck with negative cash flow still leaves you boxed in.

Positive cash flow creates options.

Negative cash flow creates pressure.

You do not need complex spreadsheets to understand this. You need awareness.

- What comes in each month?
- What goes out each month?
- What is left?

That gap—positive or negative—is your financial pace.

If you never check it, you do not know whether you are racing smart or burning out early.

Assets, Liabilities, and Net Worth

Next comes the broader picture.

Assets are things you own that have value.

Cash. Savings. Investments. Retirement accounts. Property. Businesses.

Liabilities are what you owe.

Credit cards. Student loans. Auto loans. Mortgages. Personal debt.

Net worth is assets minus liabilities.

In track terms, assets are your strengths. Liabilities are your vulnerabilities. Net worth is the full performance profile.

One strong asset does not erase multiple weaknesses. A fast final kick does not fix poor positioning for the rest of the race. You have to look at the whole event.

Many athletes confuse income with wealth.

Income is what you earn.

Net worth is what you build and keep over time.

You can have high income and low net worth if spending and debt keep pace. You can have modest income and growing net worth if decisions are disciplined.

The snapshot matters more than the highlight.

Fixed vs Variable Expenses

Not all expenses behave the same way.

Fixed expenses are relatively stable.

Rent or mortgage. Insurance premiums. Loan payments. Phone plans.

Variable expenses fluctuate.

Food. Travel. Entertainment. Convenience spending. Lifestyle choices.

In track terms, fixed expenses are your baseline training load. They define structure. Variable expenses are intensity adjustments.

Most people try to cut fixed expenses first, which is often difficult and disruptive. The real leverage usually lives in variable spending you barely notice.

Small choices repeated daily have massive impact over a season.

Coffee stops. App subscriptions. Convenience purchases. These are not dramatic, but they quietly drain momentum.

You do not need to eliminate enjoyment. You need to understand where flexibility exists.

Awareness creates control.

Reviewing Where Your Money Actually Goes

This is the film session.

It is uncomfortable.

It is revealing.

It is necessary.

Pull your bank statements. Pull your credit card statements. Look at several months, not just one. No judgment. No excuses. Just facts.

Film study is not punishment. It is how athletes improve.

You might notice:

- Subscriptions you forgot about
- Spending that does not match your priorities
- Patterns you did not realize were there
- Leaks that add up over time

If you do not watch the film, you repeat the same mistakes. Numbers do not exist to shame you. They exist to inform you.

Avoiding the snapshot does not change it.

Facing it gives you control.

Why This Step Feels So Hard

Track athletes are used to clear metrics.

Times. Splits. Rankings. Results.

Money metrics feel messier. Delayed. Less obvious. The feedback loop is longer. That makes it easier to avoid.

But avoidance has consequences.

Ignoring your financial snapshot is like refusing to look at race results because you are afraid of what they say. The data exists whether you look or not.

The athletes who improve fastest are not the most talented. They are the most honest.

Coach's Perspective

A coach would not let you guess performance.

"The numbers don't lie."

"Know your splits."

"Evaluate before you adjust."

"Details matter."

No coach builds a training plan without baseline data. Money deserves the same respect.

Before you try to run faster, you check where you are starting.

Game Situations and Decision Points

Situation 1: You feel like you are doing fine, but your account balance never grows.

Do you assume income is the problem, or review spending honestly?

Situation 2: You get a raise.

Do you upgrade lifestyle immediately, or improve cash flow first?

Situation 3: You have debt but no clear list of balances or interest rates.

Do you ignore it, or write it all down and face it?

Just like racing, progress starts with accurate assessment.

Common Athlete Mistakes and Financial Parallels

Athletes sometimes rely on feel instead of splits.

Financially, that looks like guessing instead of tracking.

Athletes avoid bad race footage.

Financially, that looks like avoiding statements.

Athletes overvalue one great race.

Financially, that looks like one big paycheck hiding poor habits.

Honest evaluation separates growth from stagnation.

Winning the Long Game

Great runners always know their pace.

They do not guess.

They do not panic.

They adjust based on data.

Your financial snapshot is not about judgment. It is about awareness. Awareness creates control. Control builds confidence.

This is how you stop running blind.

Before you change the race strategy, check the starting blocks.

Athlete Takeaways

- Know your numbers before you change your plan
- Income only matters if cash flow is positive
- Assets build strength, liabilities create drag
- Fixed expenses set structure, variable expenses offer control
- Watch the film and adjust with intention

Chapter 3: Building the Base: Budgeting and Saving

Every serious track athlete understands base training.

It is not glamorous. There are no crowds watching long runs at an easy pace. No medals are handed out for mileage logged in bad weather. But every coach knows this truth: if the base is weak, everything built on top of it collapses.

Speed comes from strength. Strength comes from consistency. Consistency comes from structure.

Money works the same way.

Budgeting and saving are not about restriction or punishment. They are base training. They are what allow you to handle pressure later, adapt to changes, and finish strong when the race gets long.

Most financial mistakes do not happen because people make reckless decisions. They happen because there is no base underneath the decision.

Why Athletes Struggle With Budgeting

Many former track athletes hear the word "budget" and immediately check out.

It sounds limiting.

It feels boring.

It feels like someone telling you what you cannot do.

That reaction comes from misunderstanding what a budget actually is.

A budget is not a set of handcuffs.

It is a training plan.

In track terms, budgeting is knowing your target pace. It tells you how fast you can go early without blowing up later. It keeps you from sprinting the first lap of a 5K and wondering why your legs are gone at mile two.

When people avoid budgeting, they are not being free. They are running blind.

Budgeting Systems That Actually Work

A budget only works if you can execute it under real-life conditions.

That means it has to be:

- Simple
- Realistic
- Repeatable

If a system requires constant attention, perfect discipline, or daily spreadsheets, it will not survive stress. Coaches do not design workouts athletes cannot complete consistently. Your money system should be no different.

At its core, a working budget answers three questions:

1. How much money comes in?
2. What must go out no matter what?
3. What is left to deploy intentionally?

That is it.

Everything else is refinement.

In track terms, this is the difference between knowing your race plan and improvising every lap. When you know the plan, decisions become easier. When you do not, every choice feels emotional.

A strong budget does not eliminate spending. It assigns purpose to spending.

Spending With Intention, Not Emotion

Many athletes do not overspend because they are careless. They overspend because spending is reactive.

You get paid.

You live your life.

You hope things work out.

That is not a plan. That is hoping fitness carries you through a race you did not prepare for.

Intentional spending means deciding ahead of time where money goes.

- What supports your life?
- What supports your goals?
- What is just noise?

This is not about cutting everything. It is about cutting what does not matter so what does matter gets protected.

The discipline you used to train transfers directly here.

Automating Savings Like Daily Mileage

No runner debates whether to do base mileage.

You do not wake up each day asking if you feel like running. You run because it is scheduled. It is part of the program. Motivation is irrelevant.

Saving should work the same way.

If you wait to save whatever is left over, you will rarely save anything. Life expands to fill available space. Convenience wins. Discipline fades.

Automation solves this.

Direct deposit into savings.

Automatic transfers on payday.

Scheduled contributions to retirement accounts.

In track terms, automation is daily mileage. You may not see dramatic results immediately, but the accumulation is powerful. Reps compound.

Automation removes emotion from the process. And emotion is where most financial mistakes live.

You are not relying on willpower. You are building a habit.

Why Saving First Changes Everything

Saving first flips the script.

Instead of spending and hoping there is something left, you protect your future upfront and adjust lifestyle around what remains.

This is how disciplined athletes operate.

You do not skip training and hope fitness shows up later. You put the work in first and enjoy the results when they come.

Saving first does not make life smaller. It makes it more secure.

Emergency Funds as Injury Protection

Every track athlete understands injury risk.

You do not plan to get hurt. You prepare anyway. Strength work. Recovery protocols. Trainers. Backup plans.

An emergency fund serves the same purpose financially.

It is cash set aside for unexpected events:

- Medical expenses
- Car repairs
- Job changes
- Delayed income
- Life disruptions

Without an emergency fund, every surprise becomes a crisis. You reach for credit. You panic. You abandon the plan.

With an emergency fund, you stay composed. You handle the situation and continue training.

In track terms, this is staying healthy enough to compete.

An emergency fund is not pessimism. It is preparation.

How Much Is Enough?

There is no perfect number.

The general goal is to build enough cash to cover several months of essential expenses. More stability and less predictable income usually require a larger buffer.

The key is not the exact amount. The key is having something.

A small emergency fund is better than none. Just like light strength work is better than skipping it entirely.

You build it gradually, the same way you build mileage.

Balancing Lifestyle With Long-Term Goals

This is where many former athletes struggle the most.

You trained hard. You sacrificed. You lived on schedules that were not your own. When money finally becomes yours, enjoying it feels justified.

That feeling is valid.

The mistake is turning short-term comfort into long-term limitation.

Track teaches delayed gratification. You run easy today so you can run fast later. You skip immediate comfort for future performance. Money requires the same mindset.

You do not have to eliminate fun. You have to be intentional.

Spend on what truly matters to you.

Reduce what does not.

Protect future options.

Lifestyle should support your life, not quietly trap it.

The Danger of Lifestyle Creep

Lifestyle creep is subtle.

Income increases. Spending increases. Nothing feels reckless. But progress stalls.

In track terms, this is adding intensity without recovery. You feel productive until you break down.

Budgets and savings prevent lifestyle creep by forcing awareness. Awareness creates choice.

Choice creates freedom.

Coach's Perspective

A coach would not sugarcoat this.

"Stick to the plan."

"Do the work when nobody's watching."

"Reps matter."

"Discipline wins races."

"Finish what you start."

Budgeting and saving are boring for the same reason base training is boring. They work.

Game Situations and Decision Points

Situation 1: You get paid.

Do you save first, or hope discipline shows up later?

Situation 2: You want to upgrade your lifestyle.

Do you check the plan, or ignore it because income feels good?

Situation 3: An unexpected expense hits.

Do you stay calm using savings, or reach for credit?

These are lap-by-lap decisions. Over time, they define outcomes.

Common Athlete Mistakes and Financial Parallels

Athletes sometimes skip base training.

Financially, that looks like skipping savings.

Athletes overestimate what their body can handle.

Financially, that looks like no emergency fund.

Athletes reward hard work with shortcuts.

Financially, that looks like lifestyle creep.

The same discipline that wins races builds financial strength.

Winning the Long Game

Budgeting and saving do not make you slower. They make you sustainable.

Control creates confidence.

Confidence reduces stress.

Reduced stress improves decision-making.

This is how you stay composed when pressure hits.

You do not win a season by sprinting every workout. You win by building a base that holds up under fatigue.

Money is no different.

Athlete Takeaways

- A budget is a training plan, not a restriction
- Save first and automate it like daily mileage
- Emergency funds keep you healthy in the long season
- Lifestyle choices today shape options tomorrow
- Build the base and trust the process

Chapter 4: Credit, Debt, and False Starts

Every track athlete knows what a false start feels like.

You are locked in. Heart rate up. Muscles ready. The gun is about to fire. Then someone twitches. The race stops. Warnings are issued. Sometimes you are disqualified before the race even begins.

False starts are not about lack of talent. They are about impatience, nerves, and poor situational awareness.

Debt works the same way.

Credit and borrowing can help you move forward when used correctly. But when they are misunderstood or rushed into, they create penalties that follow you for years. Many athletes do not lose the financial race because they are slow. They lose it because they start with deductions they never fully recover from.

Understanding credit and debt is how you avoid false starts that knock you out before momentum even builds.

Why Athletes Often Misunderstand Credit

Most athletes are never taught how credit actually works.

Growing up, bills were handled by parents. Scholarships, stipends, or team structures reduced exposure to real financial systems. When credit first shows up, it often looks like opportunity, not responsibility.

"You're approved."

"You qualify."

"You can afford it."

Those phrases sound like green lights.

In track terms, that is mistaking the crowd noise for the starter's pistol.

Approval is not permission. It is access. And access without discipline creates mistakes.

How Credit Scores and Reports Actually Work

Your credit score is not a judgment of your character. It is a performance metric.

It answers one question: how reliable are you when borrowing money?

Several factors drive that score:

- **Payment history**: Do you pay on time?
- **Credit utilization**: How much of your available credit are you using?
- **Length of credit history**: How long have you been using credit?
- **New credit**: How often do you apply for loans or cards?
- **Credit mix**: What types of credit do you use?

In track terms, your credit score is consistency over a season, not one race.

One missed payment is like clipping a hurdle. You may recover, but it costs you momentum. Repeated misses create a pattern that follows you.

Your credit report is the film. Your credit score is the result on the board. You cannot argue with it. You can only change it through disciplined reps.

Why On-Time Payments Matter More Than Anything

Paying on time is the foundation.

It matters more than income.

It matters more than how smart you are.

It matters more than potential.

Missed payments stay on your record for years. That is not punishment. That is data.

In track terms, showing up late to practice does not erase your talent. It does affect trust. Credit works the same way.

Credit Cards, Loans, and Interest

Credit cards and loans are tools.

They can help smooth cash flow.

They can help build credit history.

They can create flexibility.

They can also quietly drain your future.

Interest is the cost of borrowing. It is the opposing runner pulling away every lap you carry a balance.

The danger is not using credit. The danger is using it casually.

When balances grow, interest compounds against you. That makes recovery harder the longer you wait. It is like running into a headwind that keeps getting stronger.

Borrowing should be intentional, not convenient.

Why Minimum Payments Are a Trap

Minimum payments are designed to keep you in the race without making progress.

You stay afloat.

You feel okay.

But the balance barely moves.

In track terms, this is jogging in place while thinking you are training.

Interest keeps scoring points while you stand still.

Paying only the minimum is not neutral. It is a slow loss of position.

Good Debt vs Bad Debt

Not all debt is equal.

The difference is not the interest rate alone. It is what the debt does to your future.

Good debt generally helps build long-term capacity:

- Education that increases earning power
- Reasonably priced housing
- Business investments with a plan

Bad debt finances short-term consumption:

- Lifestyle upgrades
- Status purchases
- Convenience spending that fades quickly

In track terms, good debt is investing in training facilities or coaching. Bad debt is buying flashy gear that does not improve performance.

One builds capacity. The other adds weight.

Why Athletes Get Trapped by Debt

Athletes are confident in their ability to recover.

That confidence wins races. Financially, it can create exposure.

Common traps include:

- Using credit to support lifestyle
- Assuming future income will fix current decisions
- Ignoring balances because payments feel manageable
- Co-signing for others without understanding the risk

Debt does not care about potential. It only cares about consistency.

Once payments stack up, flexibility disappears. Decisions become reactive. Stress increases.

That is how races are lost.

Co-Signing: The Hidden Risk

Co-signing feels supportive. It feels like helping a teammate.

But co-signing means you are responsible if the other person does not pay. Missed payments affect your credit, not just theirs.

In track terms, co-signing is running someone else's leg of the relay without control over their effort.

If they drop the baton, you still lose.

Debt and Psychological Pressure

Debt does more than cost money.

It affects confidence.

It limits options.

It forces decisions.

Athletes used to performing freely often feel this pressure later, when debt limits job choices, relocation, or risk-taking.

Debt is not just financial weight. It is mental weight.

That weight shows up under stress.

Coach's Perspective

A coach would be blunt.

"Don't jump the gun."

"Know the rules."

"Protect your position."

"Smart runners finish."

"Discipline beats impulse."

Credit magnifies behavior. Handle it with respect.

Game Situations and Decision Points

Situation 1: You are approved for a credit card.

Do you use it to build discipline, or to fund convenience?

Situation 2: You qualify for a loan.

Do you ask if you should take it, or just if you can?

Situation 3: Someone asks you to co-sign.

Do you understand the risk, or feel pressured to say yes?

These are race-defining moments. Awareness matters.

Common Athlete Mistakes and Financial Parallels

Athletes sprint too early.

Financially, that shows up as over-borrowing.

Athletes ignore warnings.

Financially, that shows up as missed payments.

Athletes trust confidence over preparation.

Financially, that shows up as debt without a plan.

False starts cost races. Debt mistakes cost years.

Recovering From Debt Mistakes

If you already made mistakes, the race is not over.

Recovery requires:

- Facing the numbers honestly
- Prioritizing high-interest balances
- Making consistent, on-time payments
- Avoiding new debt while rebuilding

This is not exciting. It is effective.

In track terms, this is returning to base training after injury. Slow, disciplined progress beats reckless intensity.

Winning the Long Game

Credit is not the enemy. Poor awareness is.

Used correctly, credit builds trust and flexibility. Used emotionally, it creates penalties that linger long after the excitement fades.

The goal is not to avoid borrowing entirely. The goal is to avoid false starts that derail your race.

Smart athletes know when to push and when to hold position.

Athlete Takeaways

- Credit is consistency, not talent
- Interest works against you when discipline slips
- Borrow to build capacity, not to impress
- Co-signing puts you in someone else's lane
- Avoid false starts and stay in control of the race

Chapter 5: The Training Facility of Money: Banking Basics

Every serious track athlete knows the importance of a good training facility.

It does not have to be fancy, but it has to work. Lanes need to be marked. Equipment needs to be where it belongs. Access needs to be reliable. When the facility is disorganized, training suffers. Warm-ups take longer. Focus drops. Small frustrations pile up and distract from the work.

Your banking system is the training facility of your money.

Most athletes ignore it until something goes wrong. Fees appear. Payments miss. Cards get declined. Fraud hits. Stress spikes. Before you think about investing, growing wealth, or making big financial decisions, your banking system has to function cleanly.

If the facility is broken, everything built on top of it struggles.

Why Banking Is Foundational, Not Optional

Banking is not exciting. That is exactly why it matters.

Track success is built on boring work done well. Banking is the same. It is where money enters your life, moves through it, and gets stored for future use. A sloppy system creates friction. A clean system creates control.

Good banking does not make headlines.

Bad banking creates constant distractions.

If you are constantly reacting to overdrafts, fees, or missed payments, you are not training. You are surviving.

Checking vs Savings Accounts

Checking accounts are for movement.

Savings accounts are for storage.

Checking is where money flows in and out. Paychecks. NIL income. Rent. Groceries. Transportation. Subscriptions. Daily spending.

Savings is where money sits with purpose. Emergency funds. Short-term goals. Buffer money. Protection.

In track terms, checking is the track itself. Savings is the infield. You need both.

If all your money lives in checking, it is always in motion and always exposed. If all your money sits in savings, nothing is happening. Separation creates clarity.

Blending checking and savings into one account causes confusion and poor habits. You stop knowing what money is available to spend versus what money is protected.

Strong athletes separate training zones. Strong financial systems separate accounts.

Why You Need More Than One Account

Many athletes start with one bank account and keep it forever. That works until life gets more complex.

Multiple accounts allow you to:

- Separate spending from protection
- Reduce overdraft risk
- Create mental clarity
- Automate discipline

For example:

- One checking account for daily spending
- One savings account for emergencies
- One savings account for short-term goals

This is not complexity. It is structure.

In track terms, this is separating easy days from hard days. Everything has a purpose.

Online Banks vs Traditional Banks

Traditional banks offer:

- Physical branches
- In-person tellers
- Familiar systems

Online banks often offer:

- Lower fees
- Higher interest on savings
- Better automation tools
- Faster digital access

There is no universal right answer.

The right bank is the one that fits your system.

Some athletes value face-to-face access. Others value efficiency and automation. What matters is understanding how your bank works, what it costs, and how accessible your money is when you need it.

In track terms, this is shoe choice. Different athletes prefer different setups. What matters is fit, comfort, and reliability.

Fees Are the Quiet Performance Killer

Banking fees are like running with small weights you forgot to take off.

Individually, they do not seem dramatic. Over time, they quietly drain momentum.

Common fees include:

- Overdraft fees
- Monthly maintenance fees
- ATM fees
- Transfer fees

Most fees are avoidable with the right structure.

Automatic alerts.

Minimum balances.

Linked savings for overdraft protection.

Choosing fee-friendly institutions.

If you are paying constant fees, the problem is rarely bad luck. It is usually a broken system.

How Money Moves Electronically

Money does not move instantly or magically.

It moves through systems:

- Direct deposit
- Electronic transfers
- Debit cards
- Automatic bill pay
- ACH processing

Timing matters.

Deposits may clear in one to two days. Transfers can take several business days. Bills may pull money earlier than expected. Delays cause overdrafts. Misunderstanding timing causes stress.

In track terms, this is race timing. You do not assume splits. You know them.

Knowing when money arrives and when it leaves keeps you in control.

Direct Deposit and Automation

Direct deposit is one of the most powerful tools athletes underuse.

It allows income to:

- Enter accounts automatically
- Be split across multiple accounts
- Support saving without decision-making

For example:

- 80% to checking
- 20% to savings

Automation removes emotion. Emotion is where mistakes happen.

In track terms, this is daily mileage. You do not debate whether to run easy miles. You do them because they are part of the plan.

Protecting Yourself From Fraud

Fraud is part of modern life.

Debit cards get skimmed. Online accounts get hacked. Data gets exposed. The goal is not to eliminate risk. The goal is to detect it quickly.

Protection strategies include:

- Regularly checking accounts
- Setting transaction alerts

- Using strong, unique passwords
- Separating savings from spending
- Acting immediately on suspicious activity

Fraud is easiest to fix when caught early. Ignoring accounts creates delay, and delay increases damage.

In track terms, this is awareness during a race. You adjust when something feels off. You do not ignore it and hope it resolves itself.

Overdrafts: The Preventable Mistake

Overdrafts happen when money leaves an account with insufficient balance.

They are rarely emergencies. They are usually system failures.

Overdrafts happen because of:

- Poor timing
- No buffer
- Too many auto-payments
- No alerts

Simple fixes prevent them:

- Keep a buffer in checking
- Link savings for protection
- Use alerts
- Know bill dates

Overdraft fees are penalties for poor execution, not bad intent.

Coach's Perspective

A coach would be blunt.

"Handle your business."

"Details matter."

"Protect the facility."

"Stop creating your own problems."

No coach accepts excuses for sloppy preparation. Banking is preparation.

Game Situations and Decision Points

You use one account for everything. Do you build structure or keep guessing?

You get hit with fees. Do you adjust the system or ignore it?

You see a charge you do not recognize. Do you act immediately or wait?

These decisions feel small. Over time, they define control.

Common Athlete Mistakes and Financial Parallels

Athletes ignore details.

Financially, that shows up as fees and overdrafts.

Athletes trust systems blindly.

Financially, that leads to missed fraud.

Athletes avoid boring work.

Financially, that creates chaos.

Winning the Long Game

A clean training facility does not make you faster overnight. It allows consistent work to happen without distraction.

Good banking works the same way.

It supports everything else.

It reduces stress.

It creates clarity.

When your banking system is clean, money decisions become easier. Focus improves. Discipline becomes automatic.

That is how you train consistently and race well.

Athlete Takeaways

- Checking is for movement, savings is for protection
- Choose banks that fit your training system
- Know when money enters and exits your accounts
- Automate discipline to remove emotion
- Protect the facility so training can happen uninterrupted

Part II: Risk Management and Staying Healthy

You cannot compete if you are injured or overtrained.

Every experienced track athlete learns this lesson the hard way or the smart way.

You can be talented. You can be fast. You can be motivated. None of it matters if your body breaks down. Injuries, burnout, and overtraining do not usually come from one bad decision. They come from ignoring warning signs, pushing too hard at the wrong time, or failing to protect yourself when the workload increases.

Money works the same way.

Financial progress is not just about speed or growth. It is about staying healthy enough to stay in the race. Risk that is unmanaged does not announce itself loudly at first. It shows up quietly, then all at once, when something goes wrong and you realize you are sidelined.

Part II is about protection, awareness, and smart pacing.

This section focuses on the financial equivalents of injury prevention, recovery, and load management. Understanding risk. Knowing when to push and when to back off. Using insurance and protection tools correctly. Avoiding decisions that feel aggressive in the moment but cost you seasons later.

In track, smart athletes respect recovery days. They listen to their bodies. They understand that staying healthy over a long season matters more than one hard workout.

Financially, the same discipline applies.

You do not win by taking reckless risks.

You do not stay competitive by ignoring protection.

You do not build longevity by assuming nothing will go wrong.

Risk management is not playing scared. It is playing smart.

The chapters in this part will help you:

- Understand the difference between emotional confidence and real capacity
- Protect your income and progress from unexpected setbacks
- Use insurance and risk tools the right way, not the cheapest way
- Stay flexible so one bad event does not knock you out of the race

Strong athletes train with intention. Strong financial plans protect availability.

This is how you stay healthy, composed, and competitive for the long run.

Chapter 6: Risk Awareness and Smart Pacing

Every track athlete remembers the first time they went out too fast. The adrenaline hits. The gun goes off. You feel great through the first 100, maybe the first 200. The pace feels easy. The crowd noise feeds you. Somewhere in your head, a voice says, *I can hold this.*

Then reality shows up.

Your legs tighten. Breathing gets shallow. Form breaks down. What felt aggressive turns into survival. By the final stretch, you are no longer racing the field. You are racing fatigue and regret.

That experience teaches a lesson no stopwatch can explain.

Pacing is not about how fast you *can* go.

It is about how fast you can go *and still finish strong*.

Money works the same way.

Most financial mistakes are not caused by lack of effort or intelligence. They come from poor pacing. People push too hard when they should be steady. They take risks that feel manageable early but become overwhelming later. They confuse confidence with capacity.

Risk awareness is what keeps you from burning out financially before you reach the finish line.

Emotional Risk vs Financial Risk

Emotional risk is how you *feel* about uncertainty.

Financial risk is how much damage you can actually absorb.

Athletes often confuse the two.

You are trained to compete under pressure. You are used to discomfort. You have pushed through pain, fatigue, and doubt. That experience builds confidence, and confidence is valuable. The problem is assuming that emotional toughness automatically translates to financial resilience.

Financial risk does not care how tough you feel.

If one bad outcome would:

- Force you into high-interest debt
- Make you miss rent or mortgage payments
- Require selling investments at the worst possible time
- Push you to abandon long-term plans

Then your financial risk capacity is lower than your emotional confidence suggests.

In track terms, this is the difference between *wanting* to lead the race and being physically prepared to do it. Desire does not override physiology. Confidence does not override conditioning.

Financially, confidence does not override cash flow, savings, or flexibility.

Smart pacing starts with honest awareness of what you can handle if things do not go your way.

Time Horizon and Flexibility

Time horizon is how long your money has to work before you need it.

Short time horizon means you need stability.

Long time horizon allows for more variation.

This matters more than most people realize.

If you need money soon for:

- Living expenses
- A move
- Education
- A major purchase

You cannot afford large swings. Volatility is not just uncomfortable. It is dangerous.

If money is meant for decades in the future, short-term ups and downs matter less. You have time to recover. You can stay patient. You can let the plan work.

Flexibility is the hidden variable.

Flexibility comes from:

- Emergency savings
- Stable income
- Low fixed expenses
- Manageable debt

A runner with strong aerobic fitness and recovery can absorb a hard workout. A runner already overtrained cannot. The same workout becomes injury risk.

Financially, someone with flexibility can take calculated risks. Someone without it cannot, even if the opportunity looks good.

Before taking risk, ask:

- How soon do I need this money?
- What happens if the outcome is worse than expected?
- Do I have room to adjust?

That is pacing awareness.

How Risk Affects Every Money Decision

Risk is not just about investing.

It affects:

- How much cash you keep available
- How much debt you take on
- What insurance coverage you need
- How aggressively you upgrade lifestyle
- Whether you commit to fixed expenses

Ignoring risk does not make you bold. It makes you exposed.

Every decision carries downside. Smart athletes acknowledge it instead of pretending it does not exist.

In track terms, this is race awareness. You know the weather. You know the surface. You know your lane. You know your competition. You do not sprint blindly and hope it works out.

Financially, every decision should be filtered through one simple question:

What happens if this does not go my way?

If the answer is, *I am fine and can adjust*, the risk may be acceptable.

If the answer is, *I am stuck*, the pace is too fast.

Knowing When to Push and When to Hold Back

Great runners understand tempo.

There are moments to push:

- When you are well-prepared
- When the conditions are right
- When the payoff justifies the effort

There are moments to hold back:

- When recovery is limited
- When uncertainty is high
- When one mistake could derail the race

The mistake is racing at one speed all the time.

Financially, this shows up when people:

- Invest aggressively without savings
- Take on debt assuming income will always increase
- Make long-term commitments without flexibility
- Chase opportunities because they feel behind

Pushing at the wrong time is not courage. It is poor race management.

Smart pacing means:

- Building protection before aggression
- Increasing difficulty gradually
- Respecting recovery periods
- Adjusting strategy as conditions change

That is how you stay competitive deep into the race.

Coach's Perspective

If your coach were talking about money, the message would sound familiar.

Control what you can control.

Do not blow up the workout.

Run your race.

Stay disciplined early so you can finish strong.

Effort matters, but timing matters more.

Coaches do not reward athletes who train hard once and then disappear. They trust athletes who show up consistently and manage themselves.

Financial success works the same way.

Game Situations and Decision Points

Situation 1:

You hear about an aggressive investment with big upside.

Do you ask whether it fits your timeline and flexibility, or just whether it sounds exciting?

Situation 2:

You consider a major lifestyle upgrade.

Do you test whether your income can handle it if something changes?

Situation 3:

You feel confident and want to take more risk.

Do you check the downside, or trust momentum alone?

These are pacing decisions. The same awareness that wins races protects finances.

Common Athlete Mistakes and Financial Parallels

Athletes push through fatigue.

Financially, that looks like ignoring stress signals.

Athletes race others instead of racing their plan.

Financially, that looks like comparison-driven decisions.

Athletes assume toughness solves everything.

Financially, that leads to overexposure.

The mistakes are familiar. The consequences are just delayed.

Winning the Long Game

Risk cannot be eliminated. Burnout can be managed.

The athletes who succeed financially over decades are not the ones who sprint early. They are the ones who pace intelligently, protect themselves, and stay available.

Smart pacing is not fear.

It is professionalism.

You do not need to win today. You need to stay healthy enough to keep competing.

Athlete Takeaways

- Confidence is not conditioning. Know what you can actually handle
- Time horizon and flexibility determine how much risk makes sense
- Push when prepared. Hold back when protection matters
- Every decision has downside. Acknowledge it
- Smart pacing keeps you in the race through the finish line

Chapter 7: Insurance Fundamentals Every Athlete Needs

Every runner understands one unavoidable truth.

You can do everything right and still get hurt.

You can follow the training plan. You can warm up properly. You can hydrate, recover, and respect your limits. And still, one awkward step, one bad landing, or one unexpected strain can derail an entire season. That is not failure. That is the reality of competing in a sport where contact with the ground, repetition, and fatigue are constants.

That reality is why track athletes respect injury prevention.

You stretch even when you feel fine.

You ice things that do not hurt yet.

You follow rehab protocols even when you want to rush back.

Insurance plays the same role in your financial life.

You do not buy insurance because you expect something bad to happen. You buy it because you understand that life, like training, carries unavoidable risk. Accidents, illnesses, and unexpected events are not moral failures or planning mistakes. They are part of the environment.

Ignoring that reality does not make you disciplined.

It makes you exposed.

Insurance is not about fear. It is about staying available long enough to finish the race.

Why Insurance Is About Availability

In track, availability matters more than talent.

It does not matter how fast you are if you cannot compete. It does not matter how well training is going if one injury sidelines you for months. The best athletes are not just talented. They are consistently available.

Financially, availability works the same way.

If one unexpected event:

- Wipes out your savings
- Forces you into high-interest debt
- Derails your career plans
- Pushes you into panic decisions

Then you were not protected.

Insurance exists to keep you in the race when something unexpected happens. It absorbs impact so you do not have to abandon your plan at the first sign of adversity.

You are not paying for perfection.

You are paying for resilience.

Health Insurance Basics

Health insurance is non-negotiable.

Track athletes often feel healthy. You train hard. You recover well. You are used to pushing through discomfort. That mindset works in competition. It fails financially.

Health insurance covers:

- Doctor visits
- Prescriptions
- Imaging and diagnostics
- Surgeries

- Emergency care
- Long-term treatment

Without it, one injury or illness can erase years of progress in weeks.

In track terms, skipping health insurance is like racing without spikes on a wet track. You might get away with it for a while. When conditions change, the consequences are immediate.

Health insurance is not just for emergencies. It is about access.

Access to preventative care.

Access to early diagnosis.

Access to treatment before problems get worse.

Delayed care almost always costs more, physically and financially.

You should know:

- Your deductible
- Your out-of-pocket maximum
- What is covered and what is not
- Whether providers are in-network

Waiting until something goes wrong to learn how your plan works is like reading the meet schedule after the race starts.

Auto and Renters Insurance

Auto insurance protects more than your car.

It protects:

- You
- Passengers
- Other drivers
- Your future earnings

An accident does not just damage vehicles. It creates medical bills, legal exposure, and long-term financial risk. Without proper coverage, one mistake can follow you for years.

Renters insurance is even more misunderstood.

Many athletes skip it because they assume their belongings are not worth much. That misses the point.

Renters insurance covers:

- Personal property
- Liability if someone is injured in your home
- Temporary living expenses after a covered event

In track terms, auto and renters insurance protect your lane. One slip should not push you out of the race entirely.

These policies are usually inexpensive relative to the protection they provide. Skipping them to save a small amount of money is poor risk management.

Homeowners Insurance

If you own a home, homeowners insurance is essential.

It protects:

- The structure
- Your personal property
- Liability exposure
- Certain natural and accidental events

Owning property adds responsibility. Pipes burst. Storms happen. Accidents occur. Lawsuits appear unexpectedly.

In track terms, owning a home without insurance is like training without a safety plan. Everything feels fine until something breaks, and then the damage multiplies.

Homeowners insurance is not about predicting disaster. It is about recognizing that long-term commitments require long-term protection.

Deductibles, Premiums, and Coverage Limits

This is where confusion usually shows up.

Premiums are what you pay to keep coverage active.

Deductibles are what you pay out of pocket before insurance helps.

Coverage limits are the maximum the policy will pay.

Higher deductibles usually mean lower premiums.

Lower deductibles usually mean higher premiums.

There is no free option. There is only balance.

In track terms, this is load management. Too much intensity without recovery increases injury risk. Too little challenge limits progress.

You want:

- Premiums you can maintain consistently
- Deductibles you can handle without panic
- Coverage limits that actually protect you

Insurance is not about getting every dollar back. It is about preventing financial catastrophe.

The Danger of Being Underinsured

Many people choose the cheapest policy available.

That feels disciplined. It is often reckless.

Underinsurance works until it fails, and when it fails, it fails under pressure. Saving a small amount each month can cost you massively when something serious happens.

In track terms, this is cutting recovery to save time. It works until the injury shows up and wipes out the season.

The goal is not minimal coverage.

The goal is adequate protection.

Coach's Perspective

If a coach were talking about insurance, it would sound blunt.

Protect yourself.

Stay available.

Do not create preventable problems.

Handle your business off the track.

Coaches expect athletes to tape ankles, hydrate, and follow rehab plans. Insurance is the financial version of that responsibility.

Availability wins seasons.

Game Situations and Decision Points

Situation 1:

You feel healthy and consider skipping coverage.

Are you saving money, or borrowing risk from your future self?

Situation 2:

You choose the cheapest policy.

Do you understand what it does not cover?

Situation 3:

You assume nothing bad will happen.

Are you prepared if it does?

These decisions do not show up on a daily basis. They show up when pressure hits.

Common Athlete Mistakes and Financial Parallels

Athletes underestimate injury risk.

Financially, that leads to skipping insurance.

Athletes focus on performance, not protection.

Financially, that leads to undercoverage.

Athletes ignore details until it is too late.

Financially, that leads to surprises during emergencies.

The mistakes are familiar. The environment is just different.

Winning the Long Game

Insurance does not win races.

It keeps you eligible to compete.

You cannot control every variable. You can control preparation. Strong athletes respect defense. Strong financial plans do too.

Staying healthy financially allows you to focus on growth instead of recovery.

Athlete Takeaways

- Insurance is injury prevention for your finances
- Health coverage is non-negotiable
- Auto, renters, and homeowners insurance protect your lane
- Deductibles and premiums are trade-offs, not shortcuts
- Staying available matters more than saving a few dollars

Chapter 8: Life, Disability, and Liability Protection

Every track athlete understands one simple truth.

Your body is your engine.

Everything depends on it. Your training. Your performance. Your confidence. Your future opportunities. When the engine is healthy, you can compete. When it breaks down, everything else stops.

Most athletes think of injuries in terms of time missed. Weeks. Months. Seasons. What rarely gets discussed is the financial impact of not being able to compete, work, or earn.

That is where life, disability, and liability protection come in.

These coverages are not about pessimism. They are about protecting the engine of your financial life before something forces you to stop running.

Why Protection Beyond Health Insurance Matters

Health insurance helps pay medical bills.

It does not replace income.

It does not protect your family.

It does not shield you from lawsuits.

It does not guarantee financial stability if you cannot work.

Track teaches you to think in systems. Training is not just speed work. It includes strength, mobility, recovery, nutrition, and rest. Miss one piece, and performance suffers.

Financial protection works the same way.

Life, disability, and liability insurance exist to protect outcomes that health insurance cannot touch.

Life Insurance: Term vs Permanent

Life insurance is one of the most misunderstood tools athletes encounter.

It is not about expecting to die early.

It is about protecting people who depend on you.

If no one depends on your income today, life insurance may not feel urgent. That can change quickly with a spouse, children, or shared financial obligations.

Term Life Insurance

Term life insurance covers you for a specific period of time, often 10, 20, or 30 years.

If you pass away during that term, the policy pays a benefit to your beneficiaries. If you outlive the term, the coverage ends.

Term insurance is:

- Simple
- Affordable
- Designed for protection

In track terms, term insurance is like race-day insurance. You cover the years where risk is highest and responsibilities are greatest.

Most athletes who need life insurance need term insurance.

Permanent Life Insurance

Permanent life insurance lasts for your entire life and often includes a savings or investment component.

It is more complex.

It is more expensive.

It is often oversold.

Permanent policies can make sense in specific situations, but they are not beginner tools. Buying permanent insurance too early is like overtraining before your base is built.

Protection comes before complexity.

Disability Insurance: The Most Overlooked Coverage

If you could only choose one form of insurance besides health, disability insurance would be it.

Why?

Because your ability to earn income is your most valuable asset.

Most athletes think of disability as permanent injury. In reality, most disabilities are temporary.

Back injuries.

Stress fractures.

Surgeries.

Illness.

Chronic conditions.

Any of these can limit your ability to work for months or years.

Disability insurance replaces a portion of your income if you cannot work due to injury or illness.

In track terms, this is protecting your season when you cannot race. You may not be at full strength, but you stay in the meet.

Without disability insurance:

- Savings drain quickly

- Debt fills the gap
- Long-term plans derail

Athletes assume they will always find a way. That confidence is earned in competition. Financially, it creates risk.

Short-Term vs Long-Term Disability

Short-term disability covers shorter absences, usually weeks to months.

Long-term disability kicks in after that and can last for years or until retirement age, depending on the policy.

Employer-provided disability is common, but often incomplete.

You need to know:

- How much income is replaced
- How long benefits last
- When benefits start
- What qualifies as disability

Many athletes discover too late that coverage was limited or temporary.

Reading the policy matters.

Umbrella Liability Coverage

Umbrella insurance protects you from lawsuits that exceed the limits of your auto or homeowners insurance.

Most people assume lawsuits only happen to wealthy or reckless individuals. That is false.

Accidents escalate.

Claims grow.

Legal costs multiply.

If you injure someone in a car accident or someone is seriously hurt on your property, your basic policy may not be enough.

Umbrella coverage provides additional protection above existing policies.

In track terms, this is your final buffer. You hope never to need it, but when something breaks through, it prevents catastrophic damage.

Umbrella policies are often inexpensive relative to the protection they provide, especially for professionals, athletes, and anyone with future earning potential.

Why Athletes Underestimate Liability Risk

Athletes are conditioned to focus inward.

Training.

Performance.

Recovery.

Liability risk is external. It comes from other people, other drivers, other situations. That makes it easier to ignore.

But liability does not care how disciplined you are.

One incident can trigger years of legal and financial consequences.

Protection preserves focus.

Common Insurance Mistakes Athletes Make

Athletes do not usually make reckless mistakes. They make confident ones.

Mistake 1: Assuming youth equals safety

Health today does not eliminate risk tomorrow.

Mistake 2: Choosing the cheapest option

Cheap coverage often fails under pressure.

Mistake 3: Overbuying complex products early

Complexity without foundation creates confusion.

Mistake 4: Ignoring disability insurance

Income protection is more important than people realize.

Mistake 5: Never reviewing coverage

Life changes. Coverage should too.

These mistakes rarely hurt immediately. They show up when options disappear.

Coach's Perspective

A coach would not soften this message.

Protect the engine.

Stay available.

Do not let one setback end the season.

Prepare for what you cannot control.

Coaches plan for injuries even when athletes are healthy. Financial protection deserves the same respect.

Game Situations and Decision Points

Situation 1:

You rely only on health insurance.

What happens if you cannot work for six months?

Situation 2:

You are offered permanent life insurance early.

Do you understand the trade-offs?

Situation 3:

You have growing income and assets.

Are you protected if something goes wrong outside your control?

These decisions determine resilience, not just returns.

Winning the Long Game

Track careers teach patience, repetition, and preparation.

Financial protection works the same way.

Life insurance protects people who depend on you.

Disability insurance protects your income.

Liability insurance protects your future.

You do not win by ignoring defense. You win by staying in position long enough to finish strong.

Athlete Takeaways

- Your income is your engine. Protect it
- Term life insurance covers risk without complexity
- Disability insurance keeps you in the race if you cannot work
- Umbrella coverage protects against rare but severe setbacks
- Preparation off the track determines how long you can compete

Part III: Running Efficiently (Investing Fundamentals)

Efficiency matters more than speed.

In track, efficiency separates athletes who fade from athletes who finish strong.

Anyone can sprint for a short stretch. Anyone can look fast early. What matters is how smoothly you move, how well you manage energy, and how consistently you execute when fatigue shows up. Wasted motion costs time. Poor pacing costs races.

Investing works the same way.

This section is not about chasing fast money or flashy results. It is about building an efficient system that works mile after mile, year after year. The goal is not to win the first lap. The goal is to stay relaxed, disciplined, and in control while others burn themselves out.

Efficient investing means:

- Understanding how markets actually function
- Respecting risk instead of pretending it does not exist
- Letting compounding do the heavy lifting
- Avoiding shortcuts that feel fast but break down over time

Track athletes already understand this mindset. You do not overstride. You do not surge without purpose. You trust your training, hold your form, and let efficiency carry you through the race.

In the chapters that follow, you will learn how investing mirrors distance running:

- Stocks and bonds each play specific roles, just like different training zones
- Volatility is normal, like changes in pace and conditions
- Consistency beats intensity
- Discipline keeps you moving forward when others panic

If Part I built your base and Part II protected your health, Part III teaches you how to move efficiently once the race is underway.

This is where patience becomes an advantage.

This is where discipline turns into progress.

This is where winning stops looking dramatic and starts looking sustainable.

Efficiency is not boring.

Efficiency is how you finish.

Chapter 9: How Financial Markets Really Work

Every track athlete remembers the first time the race did not go as planned.

You trained well. You hit your splits in practice. You felt ready. Then the gun went off, the pace changed, the pack moved differently than expected, and suddenly the race felt chaotic. Someone surged early. Someone else fell back. The wind shifted. What looked predictable on paper became dynamic in real time.

The market feels the same way.

From the outside, financial markets look random. Numbers flash. Headlines scream. One day things are up, the next day they are down. Opinions come from everywhere. For athletes used to structure, that chaos feels uncomfortable.

But just like racing, the chaos is only confusing until you understand how the system works.

Markets are not random. They are competitive, adaptive, and constantly adjusting, just like a race with thousands of runners, each reacting to conditions, strategy, and fatigue.

Understanding how markets really work is the difference between reacting to every surge and running your own race.

How Financial Markets Function

At their core, financial markets exist to move capital from people who have it to businesses and governments that need it.

Companies raise money to grow.

Governments raise money to operate.

Investors provide that money in exchange for ownership or repayment.

Prices move based on expectations, not just current results.

In track terms, this is important. The market is not judging what already happened. It is reacting to what people believe will happen next. That is like a race where positioning matters as much as current speed. Athletes are constantly anticipating moves, not just responding to what already occurred.

Markets function through:

- Buyers and sellers
- Supply and demand
- Information and expectations
- Competition for returns

No single person controls the outcome. Millions of participants are making decisions simultaneously. That is why markets feel unpredictable in the short term and surprisingly consistent over the long term.

Just like races, markets reward preparation, not panic.

Stocks, Bonds, and Ownership

Understanding ownership is the foundation of investing.

When you buy stocks, you are buying ownership in real businesses. Those businesses sell products or services, hire people, compete, and try to grow profits over time. As an owner, you participate in their success and feel their struggles.

When you buy bonds, you are lending money. You are not trying to own growth. You are being paid interest in exchange for stability and predictability.

In track terms:

- Stocks are higher-intensity efforts. More upside, more variability.
- Bonds are steady aerobic work. Less exciting, but stabilizing.

You would never train only at max effort every day. You would break down. You would never train only easy miles either. You would stagnate. Successful training blends intensity and control.

Investing works the same way.

Ownership is not gambling. It is participation. You are not betting on a finish. You are running alongside businesses over time.

Market Cycles and Volatility

Markets move in cycles.

Expansion.

Slowdown.

Decline.

Recovery.

Repeat.

These cycles are not flaws. They are features of competitive systems.

Volatility is simply movement. Prices rise. Prices fall. Conditions change.

In track terms, volatility is changing pace and terrain. A headwind appears. The pack surges. The race goes tactical instead of fast. None of this means the race is broken. It means the race is happening.

Athletes who panic when conditions change make mistakes. They surge unnecessarily. They abandon their plan. They burn energy they cannot get back.

Investors make the same errors.

Volatility feels uncomfortable because it creates uncertainty. But uncertainty does not mean failure. It means the system is alive.

Permanent loss does not come from volatility. It comes from abandoning discipline, selling in panic, or forcing decisions at the wrong time.

Just like in racing, staying relaxed during uncomfortable moments is a competitive advantage.

Long-Term Strategy vs Chasing Fast Times

Every runner knows someone who looks incredible in warm-ups and early laps, then fades badly at the end.

They went out too hard.

They chased the wrong pace.

They confused speed with strategy.

Chasing fast returns works the same way.

Hot stocks.

Trending investments.

"Once-in-a-lifetime" opportunities.

Stories about someone who doubled money quickly.

These temptations feel like early surges in a race. They look impressive. They feel exciting. They often end badly.

Long-term strategy is about controlled pacing.

You do not need to win every lap.

You do not need to react to every move.

You do not need to beat everyone immediately.

You need to stay in position, conserve energy, and let time work in your favor.

Markets reward:

- Patience
- Ownership
- Consistency
- Discipline

They punish:

- Emotional reactions
- Short-term thinking
- Overconfidence
- Abandoning the plan

Fast times look good early. Strong finishes win races.

Coach's Perspective

What would a track coach say if they were talking about markets?

Stay relaxed.

Control your pace.

Do not chase every move.

Trust your training.

Finish the race.

Coaches know that panic wastes energy. They know that races are won by athletes who stay composed when others get uncomfortable.

Markets are no different.

You do not need to predict every turn.

You need to execute your plan.

You need to stay in your lane.

You need to avoid false surges.

Discipline beats excitement.

Game Situations and Decision Points

Situation 1:

The market drops sharply and headlines turn negative.

Do you abandon your strategy, or remember that volatility is part of the race?

Situation 2:

You hear about an investment that "everyone is making money on."

Do you chase the surge, or evaluate whether it fits your pace and timeline?

Situation 3:
You feel behind financially and want to make up ground quickly.
Do you force risk, or recommit to steady progress?
These are pacing decisions. Poor pacing ruins strong races.

Common Athlete Mistakes and Financial Parallels

Athletes chase early position.

Financially, that becomes chasing hot investments.

Athletes panic when the race changes.

Financially, that becomes panic selling.

Athletes abandon their race plan.

Financially, that becomes inconsistency.

The same mistakes show up in both arenas.

Winning the Long Game

Markets reward people who understand the race they are in.

You are not competing on a single day.

You are not judged by one lap.

You are not eliminated by one bad split.

You win by staying efficient, staying disciplined, and staying invested long enough for your preparation to matter.

Track teaches patience.

Track teaches pacing.

Track teaches trust in the process.

Those lessons transfer directly to investing.

Athlete Takeaways

- Markets are competitive systems, not random chaos
- Stocks and bonds are ownership and lending, not bets
- Volatility is movement, not failure

- Chasing fast returns is like sprinting too early
- Run your race, trust your training, and finish strong

Chapter 10: Risk, Return, and the Power of Compounding

Every track athlete eventually learns this lesson the hard way.

You cannot sprint the entire race.

Early in your career, it is tempting to go all out from the gun. You feel strong. Adrenaline is high. You want to separate yourself immediately. For a few seconds, it feels great. You are winning early. Then the burn sets in. Form breaks down. The finish line feels farther away than ever.

The athletes who last, who improve year after year, understand pacing.

Money works the same way.

Risk, return, and compounding are not separate concepts. They are one system. When you misunderstand one, the whole race plan breaks down. When you understand how they work together, progress starts to feel predictable instead of stressful.

This chapter is about learning how to run a financial race that finishes strong.

Risk and Reward Tradeoffs

There is no reward without risk.

In track, every training decision has a tradeoff. Speed work improves top-end performance but increases injury risk if overdone. Easy mileage builds endurance but does not sharpen race pace. Coaches balance these tradeoffs constantly.

Financially, the same rule applies.

Higher potential returns usually come with higher uncertainty.

Lower risk options usually offer more stability but slower progress.

There is no perfect option. There is only appropriate risk for your situation.

In track terms, risk is intensity. You do not run intervals at race pace every day. You layer intensity carefully, based on your season, your fitness, and your recovery capacity.

Athletes who get injured often do not lack talent. They mismanage risk. They push too hard, too often, without respecting limits.

Investors do the same thing when they chase returns without understanding downside.

Risk is not bad.

Risk is necessary.

Unmanaged risk is dangerous.

The goal is not maximum risk. The goal is sustainable progress.

Volatility vs Permanent Loss

This distinction matters more than most people realize.

Volatility is movement.

Permanent loss is damage.

Markets going up and down is normal. Prices fluctuate. Headlines change. Short-term results can look ugly even when long-term outcomes are still strong.

Permanent loss happens when you:

- Sell in panic
- Overextend and are forced to exit
- Abandon discipline
- Take risks you cannot recover from

In track terms, volatility is discomfort. It is running into the wind. It is a slow split. It is getting boxed in temporarily.

Permanent loss is injury. It is pulling a hamstring because you forced the pace. It is missing the season because you ignored warning signs.

Athletes often confuse discomfort with danger. The same mistake shows up financially.

Seeing red numbers feels bad. That does not mean something is broken. It means the race is still happening.

Permanent loss usually comes from reacting emotionally instead of sticking to the plan.

Compounding Over Time

Compounding is where everything changes.

Compounding is progress building on progress. Returns earn returns. Small gains stack. Time multiplies effort.

Athletes understand this intuitively.

You do not get fit from one workout.

You do not get faster from one season.

You do not build confidence from one race.

You get better from thousands of reps layered over time.

In track terms, compounding is aerobic base. Every easy mile matters. Individually, they feel insignificant. Collectively, they change your ceiling.

Financially, compounding works the same way.

Money invested early has more time to grow.

Growth builds on itself.

The curve accelerates later, not early.

This is why compounding is often underestimated. Early results look small. Progress feels slow. People quit too soon.

Athletes who trust the process understand that the payoff comes later.

Compounding rewards patience, not brilliance.

Why Time Is the Most Important Variable

Time is the multiplier.

You cannot shortcut it.

You cannot replace it.

You cannot recover lost time later.

Two athletes can train the same way, but the one who starts earlier has an advantage that cannot be erased.

Financially, starting earlier matters more than starting perfectly.

Waiting for confidence.

Waiting for more income.

Waiting for certainty.

Waiting for the "right moment."

All of those delays cost time. And time is what makes compounding powerful.

In track terms, skipping base training does not save time. It creates weakness that shows up later in the race.

Starting small and staying consistent beats waiting and doing nothing.

The Cost of Waiting

Waiting feels safe.

It feels responsible.

It feels cautious.

It feels smart.

It is not.

Every year you delay investing is a year compounding cannot work for you. That loss is invisible, which is why people underestimate it.

Athletes understand this with training. You cannot skip offseason work and expect to peak in season. The gap shows up when it matters most.

Financially, waiting often comes from fear of making mistakes. Ironically, waiting is often the biggest mistake.

You do not need perfect conditions.

You need participation.

Progress comes from showing up, not from timing perfection.

Coach's Perspective

What would a track coach say here?

Trust the plan.

Do not force the pace.

Reps matter.

Stack good days.

Finish strong.

Coaches know that consistency beats intensity. They know that athletes who try to win practice get hurt. The same applies financially.

You do not need to outsmart the system.

You need to stay in it.

Risk is part of training.

Recovery is part of training.

Time is part of training.

Respect all three.

Game Situations and Decision Points

Situation 1:

Markets drop and your account value declines.

Do you stop investing, or do you remember that volatility is part of the process?

Situation 2:

You feel behind financially and want to catch up fast.

Do you increase risk recklessly, or commit to disciplined progress?

Situation 3:

You keep saying you will start investing "next year."

Do you recognize the hidden cost of that delay?

Each of these moments mirrors race decisions. Poor pacing early always shows up late.

Common Athlete Mistakes and Financial Parallels

Athletes chase peak fitness too fast.

Financially, that shows up as excessive risk.

Athletes ignore recovery.

Financially, that shows up as burnout and poor decisions.

Athletes delay base work.

Financially, that shows up as lost compounding time.

The patterns repeat.

Winning the Long Game

Track careers are built over years, not races.

Financial lives are built over decades, not headlines.

Risk allows growth.

Volatility is normal.

Compounding does the heavy lifting.

The athletes who succeed long-term are not the ones who sprint early. They are the ones who manage effort, stay healthy, and trust the process long enough for results to compound.

Money rewards the same behavior.

Athlete Takeaways

- Risk and reward always move together
- Volatility is discomfort, not failure
- Permanent loss comes from poor decisions, not market movement
- Compounding rewards patience and consistency
- Start now, pace yourself, and trust the long race

Chapter 11: Stocks Without the Sprint Mentality

Every track athlete has seen this happen.

The gun goes off, and someone explodes out of the blocks like the race is only fifty meters long. They lead early. The crowd notices. For a moment, it looks impressive. Then, halfway through, their form tightens. Breathing gets shallow. Stride shortens. By the final stretch, they are hanging on while others who paced correctly are accelerating past them.

The problem was never effort.

The problem was mentality.

Stocks are often treated the same way.

People approach the stock market like a sprint. They look for quick wins, hot names, and fast results. They want excitement early. They want proof immediately. And just like in track, that mentality almost always leads to burnout, mistakes, and regret.

Stocks are not about speed.

They are about endurance, discipline, and trust in the training plan.

What Owning Stock Actually Means

When you buy a stock, you are not buying a number on a screen.

You are buying ownership.

You own a piece of a real business. That business sells products or services, hires employees, competes with other companies, manages costs, and tries to grow over time. Your results as a shareholder depend on how that business performs across years, not days.

In track terms, owning stock is committing to a season-long training cycle, not chasing one fast rep.

You do not judge your fitness after one workout.

You do not judge your career after one race.

You do not judge a business after one quarter.

Stocks reward patience because businesses grow slowly. Infrastructure is built over time. Customer bases expand gradually. Profits compound, not explode overnight.

Treating stocks like lottery tickets turns investing into gambling. Treating stocks like ownership turns investing into a long-term system.

That distinction changes everything.

Growth vs Value Investing

Growth and value investing are often framed as opposites. In reality, they are different training approaches.

Growth investing focuses on companies expected to grow faster than average. These companies often reinvest profits, expand aggressively, and attract attention. They may not look cheap. They promise future potential.

Value investing focuses on companies that appear undervalued relative to fundamentals. These companies may not be exciting. They may be overlooked. They generate steady results and often return cash to investors.

In track terms, growth investing is speed development. Explosive workouts. High upside. More strain if overdone.

Value investing is aerobic strength and efficiency. Less flash. More control. Reliable performance.

Neither approach is automatically better. Problems arise when athletes rely on only one.

A training plan built entirely on speed work leads to injury.

A plan built entirely on easy mileage limits performance.

Balanced athletes understand when to emphasize each.

Financially, a balanced portfolio often includes both growth and value. The mix should reflect your timeline, tolerance for volatility, and ability to stay disciplined when conditions change.

Dividends and Total Return

Dividends confuse a lot of athletes.

Dividends are cash payments some companies make to shareholders. They provide income while you hold the stock. Many people fixate on dividends and miss the bigger picture.

The real measure is total return.

Total return equals price growth plus dividends.

Focusing only on dividends is like focusing only on early splits. It feels concrete, but it ignores how the race finishes.

Some companies pay dividends and grow steadily.

Some companies reinvest profits and grow faster.

Both can contribute to long-term success.

In track terms, total return is the full race result. Not just the start. Not just the finish. The entire performance.

Athletes who chase dividends without understanding growth potential often sacrifice long-term progress. Athletes who ignore income entirely may miss stability when it matters.

The key is understanding role, not chasing labels.

Why Stocks Feel So Emotional

Stocks trigger emotion because they move constantly.

Prices change daily.

News cycles never stop.

Opinions are everywhere.

Track athletes understand how environment affects perception. Racing in a loud stadium feels different than training alone. Pressure amplifies emotion.

The stock market creates constant pressure. Watching prices daily is like checking your watch every fifty meters. It distracts from execution.

Successful investors do not eliminate emotion. They design systems that prevent emotion from controlling decisions.

They stop sprinting mentally.

Common Investing Myths Athletes Hear

Locker rooms and training groups are full of financial myths.

You have to trade constantly to win.

If the price drops, you failed.

You need inside information.

Stocks are just gambling.

If you are not aggressive, you are falling behind.

These myths spread because they sound confident and simple. They also align with sprint mentality.

Track punishes sprint mentality in long races. Stocks punish it too.

Trading constantly increases mistakes.

Price drops are part of normal movement.

Inside information is illegal and unnecessary.

Ownership is not gambling.

Aggression without discipline leads to collapse.

Stocks reward athletes who understand pacing, not adrenaline.

Volatility Is Not a Signal to Quit

Volatility is normal.

Markets move up and down. Businesses face challenges. Economic cycles repeat. None of this means the system is broken.

In track terms, volatility is uneven terrain or wind. It changes conditions, not the race itself.

Athletes who panic mid-race break form. Investors who panic mid-cycle lock in losses.

Permanent damage usually comes from reaction, not movement.

The ability to stay invested through volatility is a competitive advantage.

Coach's Perspective

What would your coach say?

Control what you can control.

Do not sprint the first lap.

Trust the plan.

Reps matter.

Finish strong.

No coach builds a championship runner by chasing fast splits in training. They build systems that hold up under fatigue.

Stocks require the same respect.

You do not need to win today.

You need to stay in the race.

Game Situations and Decision Points

Situation 1:

A stock you own drops sharply.

Do you panic, or revisit why you own it in the first place?

Situation 2:

You hear about a hot stock everyone is talking about.

Do you chase it emotionally, or evaluate whether it fits your plan?

Situation 3:

You feel bored with steady progress.

Do you trade for excitement, or trust compounding?

These decisions mirror race choices. Sprinting early always feels good until it does not.

Common Athlete Mistakes and Financial Parallels

Athletes sprint too early.

Financially, that looks like chasing hot stocks.

Athletes abandon pacing plans.

Financially, that looks like panic selling.

Athletes overestimate instinct.

Financially, that looks like ignoring fundamentals.

The mistakes repeat because the mindset repeats.

Winning the Long Game

Stocks are not shortcuts.

They are tools for long-term ownership and growth. When used with discipline, they compound quietly. When used emotionally, they create stress.

The athletes who succeed financially are not the ones with perfect timing. They are the ones who stay invested, manage risk, and avoid self-inflicted mistakes.

Endurance wins.

Athlete Takeaways

- Owning stock means owning a real business
- Growth and value are different training tools, not opposing teams
- Dividends matter, but total return tells the real story
- Volatility is part of the race, not a reason to quit
- Pace yourself, trust the plan, and finish strong

Chapter 12: Bonds and Holding Your Pace

Every experienced runner learns this lesson the hard way.

You feel good early. Your breathing is controlled. Legs are fresh. Everything tells you to push harder. But if you surge too aggressively without respecting the distance, you pay for it later. Form breaks down. Stride shortens. The pace you thought you could hold slips away.

Great runners do not run every race at max effort from the gun.

They understand pace.

Bonds exist in a financial plan for the same reason pacing exists in a race. They are not there to impress. They are there to help you finish.

How Bonds Work

At the most basic level, a bond is a loan.

You lend money to a borrower, usually a government or a company. In return, they agree to pay you interest and return your original money at a set date.

That is it.

There is no ownership like with stocks. You are not betting on explosive growth. You are agreeing on predictable terms.

In track terms, bonds are tempo runs.

They are controlled.

They are planned.

They build durability.

You do not expect a tempo run to set a personal record. You expect it to strengthen your system so you can handle harder efforts later.

Bonds function the same way in a portfolio. They provide structure and reliability. They are not exciting, but they matter.

Why Bonds Exist in the First Place

Many athletes struggle with bonds because they compare everything to speed.

Stocks feel like racing.

Bonds feel like jogging.

That comparison misses the point.

A complete training plan includes easy days, tempo days, and race efforts. Remove any one of those, and performance suffers.

Bonds serve several purposes:

They generate income through interest

They reduce overall volatility

They provide liquidity and stability

They help you stay invested during stressful periods

In financial terms, bonds help smooth the ride. In track terms, they help you stay on pace when conditions change.

Interest Rate Risk Explained Simply

Interest rate risk sounds complicated, but the concept is straightforward.

When interest rates rise, existing bonds become less attractive, because new bonds pay more. As a result, older bonds drop in value. When interest rates fall, existing bonds become more valuable.

This does not mean bonds are broken. It means their value moves differently than stocks.

In track terms, this is like running into a headwind or tailwind. You did not change your effort, but conditions changed around you.

If you hold a bond to maturity, you still receive the interest and principal as promised, assuming the borrower does not default. Temporary price movement matters less when your plan is long-term.

The mistake athletes make is judging bonds by short-term movement instead of purpose.

Credit Risk and Trust

Credit risk refers to the borrower's ability to pay you back.

A government bond issued by a stable country carries low credit risk. A bond issued by a struggling company carries higher credit risk.

Higher risk usually means higher interest, but also higher chance of problems.

In track terms, credit risk is trusting your training partner.

A reliable partner shows up, runs the workout as planned, and finishes strong. A risky partner skips sessions, pushes unpredictably, and may leave you hanging.

You choose your partners based on the workout goal. Bonds work the same way. Safety has value.

When Bonds Make Sense

Bonds are not an all-or-nothing decision.

They tend to matter more in certain situations:

When you are closer to needing your money

When income stability matters

When market volatility affects your behavior

When protecting progress is as important as growing it

Early in your career, you may rely more heavily on growth assets. As your timeline shortens, bonds often play a bigger role.

This is not about fear. It is about realism.

In track, you would not train for a marathon the same way you train for a

400-meter dash. Different events require different emphasis.

Your financial event changes over time.

Bonds as Shock Absorbers

One of the most underappreciated roles of bonds is behavioral.

During market downturns, stocks can fall sharply. Emotion rises. Stress increases. Decision-making suffers.

Bonds often decline less, or even rise, during those periods. That stability helps you stay disciplined.

In track terms, bonds are the steady rhythm that keeps you from blowing up when the race gets uncomfortable.

Many investors do not fail because their strategy was bad. They fail because they abandoned it under pressure. Bonds help reduce that risk.

Bonds in a Diversified Portfolio

Diversification means combining assets that behave differently.

Stocks and bonds often move in different directions. When one struggles, the other may hold steady.

This matters because investing success is not just about return. It is about survivability.

A portfolio that grows fast but collapses emotionally is not useful. A portfolio that allows you to stay invested through cycles wins over time.

In track terms, diversification is cross-training.

You do not build durability by doing only one type of workout. You mix stress and recovery. Strength and speed. Effort and control.

Bonds add control.

Common Bond Misconceptions

Athletes often hear:

Bonds are for old people

Bonds are dead

Bonds do not make money

Bonds are boring

All of those may be partially true, and completely irrelevant.

Boring is not bad.

Old is not an insult.

Stability is not weakness.

No coach criticizes an athlete for running controlled splits. They criticize athletes who lose discipline.

Coach's Perspective

What would your coach say?

Hold your pace.

Do not surge without a reason.

Stay relaxed.

Trust the training.

Finish the race.

Bonds exist to help you execute, not to excite you.

Game Situations and Decision Points

Situation 1:

Markets drop sharply.

Do you panic, or lean on stability to stay invested?

Situation 2:

You are approaching a major financial goal.

Do you risk volatility, or prioritize protection?

Situation 3:

You feel impatient with steady progress.
Do you abandon balance, or trust compounding?
Each choice mirrors race execution.

Common Athlete Mistakes and Financial Parallels

Athletes surge early.
Financially, that means ignoring stability.
Athletes chase competitors instead of splits.
Financially, that means chasing returns instead of goals.
Athletes abandon the plan under fatigue.
Financially, that means panic selling.
The pattern is familiar.

Winning the Long Game

Bonds are not about winning today.

They are about finishing the season healthy, consistent, and confident.

The athletes who succeed financially understand that speed without control leads to collapse. Bonds help you manage effort, preserve gains, and stay in position for long-term success.

You do not need to run every step at max speed.

You need to run smart.

Athlete Takeaways

- Bonds are pacing tools, not performance highlights
- Interest rate and credit risk are part of the course
- Bonds matter more as timelines shorten
- Stability helps you stay disciplined under pressure
- Holding your pace wins more races than sprinting early

Chapter 13: Funds, ETFs, and Team-Based Investing

Every runner eventually learns a hard truth.

No one wins a season alone.

Even the most talented athlete depends on coaches, training partners, support staff, and systems that make consistent performance possible. Relays are obvious examples, but even individual events rely on team structure behind the scenes. When everything works together, effort goes further. When it does not, talent gets wasted.

Funds and ETFs exist for the same reason.

They are team-based investing tools designed to reduce mistakes, increase consistency, and help you stay in the race longer without having to do everything yourself.

Why Team-Based Investing Exists

Many athletes are drawn to individual stock picking because it feels like racing solo.

You pick the lane.

You control the pace.

You own the outcome.

That sounds appealing, but it comes with risk.

Individual investing requires time, research, emotional discipline, and constant decision-making. Miss one detail, and the cost can be real. Most people do not fail because they are lazy. They fail because managing everything alone under pressure is hard.

Team-based investing spreads the workload.

In track terms, this is training within a program instead of guessing workouts on your own. You still work hard, but the structure protects you from avoidable mistakes.

What Mutual Funds and ETFs Actually Are

Mutual funds and ETFs are collections of investments bundled together.

Instead of owning one stock or bond, you own a slice of many.

That means:

Less reliance on any single outcome

More consistent performance

Reduced volatility

Built-in diversification

Think of this like running with a pack.

You are not relying on one stride to win the race. You are letting rhythm and consistency carry you forward.

Mutual Funds vs ETFs

Both mutual funds and ETFs pool investor money to buy diversified assets. The difference is how they operate.

Mutual Funds

Mutual funds are typically bought and sold at the end of the day at a set price. They often require minimum investments and may be actively managed.

In track terms, mutual funds are structured training plans.

They are controlled.

They are supervised.

They follow a defined process.

You do not adjust them mid-session. You trust the system to execute over time.

ETFs

ETFs trade throughout the day like stocks. They often have lower minimums and are commonly used for passive investing.

In track terms, ETFs are tempo workouts with flexibility.

You still follow structure, but you have more control over timing and execution.

Neither is better by default. The right choice depends on simplicity, cost, access, and behavior.

Index vs Active Strategies

This is one of the most misunderstood debates in investing.

Index Investing

Index funds aim to match the performance of a market index. They do not try to outsmart the market. They try to stay consistent.

In track terms, index investing is running your race.

You focus on your splits.

You trust training.

You do not react to every competitor move.

Index strategies emphasize discipline over prediction.

Active Investing

Active funds try to outperform the market through research, timing, and selection.

In track terms, this is racing tactically.

You surge.

You respond.

You adjust strategy mid-race.

Active investing can work, but it depends heavily on execution and cost. Many active strategies fail to justify their complexity over time.

The key question is not which sounds better. It is which you can stick with under pressure.

Why Fees Matter More Than Most Athletes Realize

Fees are small numbers with big consequences.

Expense ratios are the cost of running a fund. They may look insignificant, but they compound over time.

A difference of half a percent may not feel like much today. Over decades, it can cost tens or hundreds of thousands of dollars.

In track terms, fees are friction.

Poor shoes.

Bad surface.

Sloppy form.

Each one seems minor. Together, they slow you down.

The problem with fees is they are guaranteed. Returns are not. Every dollar paid in fees is a dollar that cannot compound for you.

Diversification Without Complexity

One of the biggest advantages of funds and ETFs is simplicity.

You do not need to analyze every company.

You do not need to predict markets.

You do not need to rebalance constantly.

Diversification spreads risk across industries, geographies, and asset types.

In track terms, diversification is cross-training.

You build strength without overloading one muscle group. You reduce injury risk. You improve durability.

Complexity feels productive. Simplicity performs better under stress.

Behavioral Advantages of Team-Based Investing

Most financial mistakes are emotional.

Chasing performance.

Panicking during downturns.

Overconfidence after wins.

Abandoning plans mid-cycle.

Funds and ETFs reduce the number of decisions you have to make. Fewer decisions mean fewer chances to make mistakes.

In track, fewer races often lead to better performance. You do not race every weekend at max effort. You choose moments intentionally.

Team-based investing protects your discipline.

Coach's Perspective

What would your coach say?

Trust the system.

Do not freelance.

Reps matter.

Consistency wins.

Do not overthink simple work.

Funds and ETFs are not shortcuts. They are tools that allow consistent execution.

Game Situations and Decision Points

Situation 1:

You want exposure to the market but lack time to research.

Do you go solo or join a team?

Situation 2:

You see a hot stock trending.

Do you chase it or stay diversified?

Situation 3:

Markets are volatile.

Do you react emotionally or stick to the plan?

Each decision reflects discipline.

Common Athlete Mistakes and Financial Parallels

Athletes overestimate individual impact.

Financially, that means stock picking without experience.

Athletes ignore recovery.

Financially, that means ignoring fees and friction.

Athletes abandon systems when results lag.

Financially, that means switching strategies too often.

The outcome is predictable.

Winning the Long Game

Funds and ETFs are not flashy.

They do not promise shortcuts.

They do not guarantee wins.

They do not make headlines.

They do something better.

They help you stay consistent long enough for compounding to work.

Track careers reward patience, repetition, and execution. Investing does too.

You do not need to outrun everyone today.

You need to stay in the race.

Athlete Takeaways

- Team-based investing reduces mistakes and stress
- Mutual funds and ETFs provide structure and flexibility
- Index strategies reward discipline over prediction
- Fees quietly affect long-term results

- Consistency beats complexity every season

Chapter 14: Real Estate and Alternative Events

Every track athlete understands specialty events.

Not everyone runs the same race. Some athletes thrive in sprints. Others excel in distance. Some train for hurdles, jumps, or throws. These events exist for a reason. They add opportunity. They reward specific skill sets. But no coach puts an athlete into a specialty event before they have built a base.

Real estate and alternative investments work the same way.

They are not the starting blocks. They are not base mileage. They are specialty events that can add value when timed correctly and executed with discipline. Used too early, or without understanding, they create strain instead of progress.

Why Athletes Are Drawn to Real Estate and Alternatives

Athletes are conditioned to look for edges.

Better shoes.

Smarter training plans.

New recovery tools.

That mindset often carries into money.

Real estate and alternatives are frequently framed as "how real wealth is built." They sound sophisticated. They feel tangible. They come with stories of big wins and passive income. That combination makes them attractive, especially to athletes who are confident in their ability to work through challenges.

The problem is timing.

In track terms, this is signing up for a steeplechase before you have built aerobic capacity. The event itself is not the issue. The lack of preparation is.

Renting vs Owning

Renting and owning are often framed as opposites. One is praised. The other is criticized. That framing is misleading.

Renting

Renting offers flexibility.

You can relocate easily.

You are not responsible for maintenance.

Your costs are more predictable.

You preserve mobility during career changes.

In track terms, renting is base training.

It allows movement.

It supports adaptation.

It keeps options open.

Renting is not falling behind. It is often the smart move early in a career or during transitions.

Owning

Owning offers long-term potential.

You build equity.

You control the environment.

You gain stability over time.

But ownership also brings responsibility.

Maintenance.

Repairs.

Property taxes.

Insurance.

Illiquidity.

In track terms, owning is committing to a long-distance race.

You need preparation.

You need pacing.

You need staying power.

Buying too early is like racing a marathon without long runs. You might finish, but the damage adds up.

The Hidden Costs of Ownership

Most people focus on the upside of owning and underestimate the load.

Ownership ties up capital.

Unexpected expenses happen.

Selling takes time.

Market conditions matter.

When income changes or life shifts, real estate becomes harder to adjust than most investments.

That does not make it bad. It makes it demanding.

Specialty events demand respect.

REITs and Indirect Ownership

REITs allow you to invest in real estate without owning property directly.

You gain exposure to real estate through publicly traded vehicles that own income-producing properties. You do not manage tenants. You do not fix roofs. You do not negotiate leases.

In track terms, REITs are relay legs.

You participate in the event without carrying the entire race yourself.

REITs can provide:

Income

Diversification

Liquidity compared to direct property

They also come with market risk. Prices move. Income can fluctuate. They are still investments, not guarantees.

For many athletes, REITs make more sense earlier than direct ownership because they preserve flexibility while providing exposure.

Alternatives Like Commodities and Private Investments

Alternatives include assets outside traditional stocks and bonds.

Commodities.

Private equity.

Private credit.

Hedge strategies.

Other non-traditional investments.

They can diversify portfolios and provide unique return drivers. They also introduce complexity.

Alternatives are often:

Illiquid

Hard to value

Expensive

Difficult to exit

Opaque

In track terms, these are niche events.

They require specialized training.

They punish mistakes.

They magnify execution errors.

Most athletes do not need alternatives early. Fundamentals produce better results than complexity.

Why Alternatives Are Often Misused

Alternatives appeal to identity.

They feel advanced.

They sound exclusive.

They promise access.

This creates pressure to participate before readiness.

In track, this is running elite meets without qualifying times. The environment exposes weaknesses quickly.

Alternatives should complement a strong foundation, not compensate for a weak one.

Liquidity and Risk Considerations

Liquidity is how quickly you can access money without penalty or delay.

Stocks and bonds are generally liquid.

Real estate and alternatives often are not.

Illiquidity matters when life changes.

Job transitions.

Injuries.

Family needs.

Unexpected expenses.

In track terms, liquidity is race flexibility.

If conditions change mid-race, can you adjust pace or are you locked in?

Before committing to illiquid investments, ask:

When might I need this money?

What happens if income changes?

How long am I willing to be locked in?

Ignoring liquidity creates pressure. Pressure leads to mistakes.

Risk Is Not Just About Returns

Risk is often framed as volatility. That is incomplete.

Real risk is being forced into bad decisions.

Selling at the wrong time.

Borrowing at high cost.

Sacrificing long-term goals to solve short-term problems.

Illiquid assets increase the chance of forced decisions.

Strong athletes plan for fatigue. Strong financial plans plan for stress.

Coach's Perspective

What would your coach say?

Build the base first.

Know the event.

Respect the distance.

Do not rush readiness.

Execute when it fits.

Real estate and alternatives belong in the plan only when the foundation can support them.

Game Situations and Decision Points

Situation 1:

You want to buy property because others are doing it.

Do you assess readiness or follow the crowd?

Situation 2:

You hear about a private deal with limited access.

Do you understand liquidity and risk or chase urgency?

Situation 3:

You feel bored with steady progress.

Do you add complexity or stay disciplined?

The right answer depends on timing, not ego.

Common Athlete Mistakes and Financial Parallels

Athletes rush specialization.

Financially, that means premature real estate or alternatives.

Athletes underestimate recovery.

Financially, that means ignoring liquidity.

Athletes chase prestige events.

Financially, that means complexity without readiness.

The result is strain instead of progress.

Winning the Long Game

Real estate and alternative investments are not shortcuts.

They are events that reward preparation, patience, and execution.

Used correctly, they can strengthen a plan. Used emotionally, they destabilize it.

Track success comes from pacing, not panic. Financial success works the same way.

Athlete Takeaways

- Renting and owning are strategic choices, not status symbols
- REITs offer real estate exposure with flexibility
- Alternatives add complexity and demand readiness
- Liquidity protects you when conditions change
- Build the base before entering specialty events

Part IV: Race Strategy and Adjustments

Winning requires awareness, not panic.

Every experienced runner knows this know this phase of the race feels different.

The base has been built. Fitness is there. You are no longer thinking about whether you can finish. Now the focus shifts to *how* you finish. Pace awareness matters. Small adjustments matter. Panic ruins races that preparation could have won.

Money works the same way.

Once the fundamentals are in place, success is no longer about doing more or reacting faster. It is about staying aware, making measured adjustments, and trusting the training you already put in. This is where many athletes struggle, not because they lack discipline, but because pressure increases and emotions get louder.

Part IV is about execution under stress.

You are no longer learning what money is. You are learning how to manage it when markets move, life changes, and emotions try to hijack decisions. This is the phase where overreactions do the most damage. A runner who surges too early fades. An investor who panics or overcorrects gives away progress.

Race strategy in track is situational.

You read the field.

You feel your breathing.

You monitor splits.

You adjust without abandoning the plan.

Financial strategy demands the same mindset.

Markets fluctuate. Careers evolve. Goals shift. The mistake is reacting to every noise instead of making deliberate adjustments. The athletes who finish strong are not the ones who sprint every lap. They are the ones who stay composed, reassess calmly, and keep moving forward with purpose.

This section focuses on:

- Allocating assets with lane discipline
- Buying and holding with confidence
- Rebalancing without overcorrecting
- Managing the mental side of pressure and comparison

These chapters are about staying steady when the race tightens.

You do not win by panicking.

You win by executing.

Part IV teaches you how to stay in control when it matters most, so when the final stretch arrives, you are not scrambling. You are ready.

Chapter 15: Asset Allocation and Lane Discipline

Every track athlete learns this lesson early.

Your lane is your responsibility.

You cannot drift into someone else's lane. You cannot panic and cut across the track. You cannot chase what another runner is doing three lanes over. If you do, you get disqualified or you burn energy correcting mistakes you never needed to make.

Winning races is not just about speed. It is about discipline. Staying in your lane. Running your race. Trusting the plan.

Asset allocation is lane discipline for money.

It is how you decide *where* your money runs. Stocks. Bonds. Cash. Domestic. International. Growth. Stability. Each piece has a role. When those roles are clear, your financial race stays controlled. When they are not, confusion and overreaction creep in.

Most financial mistakes are not caused by bad investments. They are caused by poor allocation and emotional lane changes.

Opening Story From the Sport

Think about the first time you raced someone faster than you.

Maybe it was a conference meet. Maybe nationals. You knew their reputation. You heard the crowd react when they were announced. The temptation was strong to match their pace early. To surge. To prove something.

And then it happened.

You went out too fast. Your breathing tightened. Your stride shortened. By the third lap, the race felt longer than it ever had. The runner you chased stayed smooth. You faded.

Your fitness did not fail you. Your discipline did.

Asset allocation works the same way. When you abandon your lane and chase what looks impressive, you sacrifice control. Control is what gets you to the finish line strong.

What Asset Allocation Really Means

Asset allocation is how your money is divided among different types of investments.

Stocks for growth.

Bonds for stability.

Cash for flexibility.

It is not about picking winners. It is about positioning.

In track terms, asset allocation is deciding whether you are running a sprint, middle distance, or long-distance race. Each event requires a different strategy. No one trains a marathon runner like a 100-meter sprinter. Money should not be treated any differently.

Financially, this works the same way as training cycles.

You do not sprint the entire season. You build a base. You layer intensity. You adjust volume and recovery based on timing. Asset allocation is that long-term structure.

Stocks, Bonds, and Cash: Knowing Each Role

Stocks are your engine.

They provide long-term growth. They fluctuate. They feel uncomfortable at times. But over long periods, they are what move you forward.

In track terms, stocks are aerobic capacity. They take time to develop.

They look slow early. They win late.

Bonds are your stabilizers.

They do not deliver explosive growth, but they reduce volatility. They smooth the ride when markets get rough. They keep you from falling apart during tough stretches.

In track terms, bonds are pacing control. They keep you from blowing up.

Cash is your flexibility.

It is not there to win the race. It is there to give you options. Emergencies. Opportunities. Transitions.

In track terms, cash is recovery. You cannot race hard without it.

The mistake athletes make is overvaluing one role and ignoring the others. A runner who only sprints burns out. A portfolio that only chases growth creates stress and bad decisions.

Domestic vs International: Expanding Your Track

Many athletes assume home turf is safer.

Domestic investments feel familiar. You know the companies. You hear the headlines. That comfort creates bias.

But the global economy is one race.

International investments expose you to growth in other regions, currencies, and markets. They add diversification and reduce reliance on any one country's performance.

In track terms, this is racing beyond your local circuit.

You get stronger when you face different conditions. Different tracks. Different competition. Staying only local limits development.

International exposure does not mean abandoning home. It means acknowledging that opportunity exists everywhere.

Diversification: Staying Balanced Across Lanes

Diversification means spreading risk across different investments.

It does not mean owning everything.

It does not mean complexity.

It means balance.

In track terms, diversification is not relying on one strength to carry you. Speed alone does not win distance races. Endurance alone does not win sprints. You train all systems so one weakness does not derail you.

Financially, diversification protects against surprises.

Markets rotate. Leaders change. Entire sectors fall out of favor. When all your money is in one lane, one stumble can end the race.

Diversification keeps mistakes from becoming catastrophic.

Career-Stage Allocation: Your Race Changes Over Time

No athlete runs the same race forever.

Early career is about development.

Mid-career is about execution.

Late career is about preservation and transition.

Your asset allocation should reflect that.

Early on, you generally have more time. More ability to recover from mistakes. More tolerance for volatility. That often means a higher allocation to growth.

As you move through your career, responsibilities increase. Families. Mortgages. Career shifts. That calls for more balance and stability.

Later, protecting what you built becomes more important than chasing what you might gain.

In track terms, this is knowing when to race aggressively and when to race smart.

The biggest mistake athletes make is never adjusting. They keep sprinting long after the race demands pacing.

Coach's Perspective

What would your coach say?

"Run your race."

"Stay in your lane."

"Do not chase noise."

"Trust the plan."

"Discipline beats talent when talent panics."

Coaches know something investors forget.

You do not win races by reacting to every move. You win by executing your strategy with discipline.

Asset allocation is not about excitement. It is about control.

Game Situations and Decision Points

You hear about a hot stock or sector.

Do you abandon your allocation or stick to your lane?

Markets drop sharply.

Do you panic and change strategy or trust your long-term positioning?

Your income increases.

Do you rebalance responsibly or overexpose yourself to risk?

These moments decide outcomes.

Common Athlete Mistakes and Financial Parallels

Athletes chase faster runners.

Financially, that means chasing performance.

Athletes go out too fast.

Financially, that means taking too much risk early.

Athletes ignore recovery.

Financially, that means no cash or stability.

The race always punishes impatience.

Winning the Long Game

Asset allocation is not about brilliance.

It is about discipline.

The athletes who finish strong are not the ones who surged early. They are the ones who stayed controlled, adjusted intelligently, and trusted their training.

Money rewards the same behavior.

Stay in your lane.

Make adjustments on purpose.

Trust the plan.

Finish strong.

Athlete Takeaways

- Run your race, not someone else's splits
- Stocks grow, bonds stabilize, cash protects
- Diversification keeps one mistake from ending the race
- Your allocation should evolve as your career changes
- Discipline wins more races than speed

Chapter 16: Buying, Holding, and Trusting the Training Plan

Every serious runner believes in a training plan.

You do not just show up and run hard every day. You follow mileage. You respect recovery. You trust the workouts even when progress feels slow. You know that skipping steps or changing plans mid-cycle usually leads to injury, burnout, or plateau.

Investing works the same way.

Most people do not fail financially because they pick the wrong investment. They fail because they abandon the plan. They panic. They tinker. They react to noise. They stop trusting the training when the race gets uncomfortable.

Buying, holding, and trusting the plan is how you finish strong.

Opening Story From the Sport

Think about the middle of a long training cycle.

You are tired. Legs feel flat. Splits are not improving. Someone else on the team seems to be flying. Doubt creeps in. You start questioning everything.

"Should I add more speed work?"

"Should I cut mileage?"

"Maybe this plan is not working."

Great athletes resist that urge.

They check the fundamentals. Sleep. Nutrition. Consistency. Then they stick with the plan.

Financially, markets create the same moment. Progress feels slow. Volatility shows up. Headlines scream urgency. The temptation is to change everything.

That is when discipline matters most.

Opening and Funding Accounts: Setting Up the Training Environment

Before training starts, you need the right environment.

Shoes that fit.

A track that is accessible.

A schedule that works.

Financial accounts are your training environment.

Brokerage accounts, retirement accounts, and savings vehicles are simply places where money lives and works. Opening them is not complicated, but avoiding them delays progress.

The biggest mistake athletes make is waiting for perfect timing. Perfect knowledge. Perfect confidence.

In track terms, this is waiting for perfect weather before training. It never happens.

You open accounts so you can start training. You fund them so the work can begin. You do not need maximum contributions on day one. You need consistency.

Financially, this works the same way as building mileage. Start where you are. Increase gradually. Stay consistent.

Market Orders vs Limit Orders: Execution Matters

In races, execution matters as much as preparation.

A market order is like stepping on the line and running when the gun fires. You accept the pace as it is. You get moving immediately.

A limit order is like waiting for a specific moment to surge. You want a precise condition before you act.

Both can work.

Market orders prioritize participation. Limit orders prioritize precision.

The mistake athletes make is overthinking execution instead of focusing on consistency. They obsess over the perfect entry point instead of staying in the race.

In long-term investing, participation matters more than perfection. Missing the race entirely because you are waiting for ideal conditions is worse than starting imperfectly.

The market does not reward hesitation.

Buy-and-Hold Discipline: Trusting the Long Build

Buy-and-hold investing means owning assets for long periods of time and allowing compounding to work.

This is not passive laziness. It is active discipline.

In track terms, buy-and-hold is base training.

You run miles that do not feel impressive. You repeat workouts that look boring. You stack weeks and months. Over time, fitness shows up.

Athletes understand that gains are delayed. Financially, people forget that.

They want confirmation immediately. They want reassurance every week. Markets do not work that way.

Businesses grow slowly. Economies expand unevenly. Progress shows up over years, not days.

Buy-and-hold works because it aligns with reality, not emotion.

Why Trading Feels Tempting and Fails Athletes

Trading feels like speed work.

Fast. Intense. Exciting.

It gives the illusion of control. You are doing something. Making moves. Staying active.

But most athletes do not benefit from excessive speed work. It increases injury risk and distracts from aerobic development.

Financially, frequent trading does the same thing.

It increases costs.

It increases taxes.

It increases stress.

It increases mistakes.

Markets punish overactivity. Just like bodies punish overtraining.

The athletes who succeed financially treat investing like endurance training, not sprint drills.

Avoiding Emotional Decisions: Running Through Discomfort

Markets will test you.

Prices will drop.

Headlines will scare you.

Friends will brag.

Fear and greed will pull you in opposite directions.

Emotional decisions feel urgent. They rarely improve outcomes.

In track terms, this is hitting the wall and panicking. You tighten up. Your form collapses. You waste energy fighting discomfort instead of managing it.

Emotion is not the enemy. Reaction is.

You acknowledge fear. You do not let it dictate decisions.

The plan exists to protect you from yourself when pressure rises.

Coach's Perspective

What would your coach say?

"Trust the training."

"Stick to the plan."

"Do not make emotional decisions."

"Control what you can control."

"Next rep."

Coaches know that athletes fail when they abandon structure under pressure. Financial discipline works the same way.

The plan only works if you execute it when it is uncomfortable.

Game Situations and Decision Points

Markets drop sharply.

Do you stop investing or keep showing up?

You hear about a hot opportunity.

Do you chase it or evaluate if it fits your plan?

You feel behind.

Do you force risk or trust long-term progress?

Every decision is a rep. Reps shape outcomes.

Common Athlete Mistakes and Financial Parallels

Athletes change plans mid-cycle.

Financially, that means abandoning strategy.

Athletes chase teammates' workouts.

Financially, that means chasing performance.

Athletes panic during fatigue.

Financially, that means selling at the worst time.

The same habits that derail training derail investing.

Winning the Long Game

Great runners are not reckless.

They are disciplined.

They trust their training even when results lag. They understand that progress compounds. They accept discomfort as part of growth.

Financial success works the same way.

You do not need perfect timing.

You do not need constant action.

You need consistency, patience, and discipline.

Buy well.

Hold patiently.

Trust the plan.

Finish strong.

Athlete Takeaways

- Open accounts and start training, even if conditions are not perfect
- Participation beats perfect timing
- Buy-and-hold is base training for wealth
- Emotional reactions ruin execution
- Trust the plan when the race gets uncomfortable

Chapter 17: Rebalancing and Mid-Race Adjustments

Every experienced runner knows this truth.

No race goes exactly as planned.

The pace feels different than expected. Weather changes. Someone surges early. Your legs feel heavier or lighter than they did in training. What separates strong racers from frustrated ones is not perfection. It is adjustment without panic.

Rebalancing works the same way in money.

You do not rebalance because something went wrong. You rebalance because movement is normal. Markets shift. Investments drift. Life changes. If you never adjust, small imbalances turn into big problems. If you adjust too often, you exhaust yourself and lose rhythm.

The goal is simple. Stay aligned with your plan while the race unfolds.

Opening Story From the Sport

Think about a long-distance race where the opening mile goes out too fast.

Adrenaline is high. The pack is tight. The pace feels manageable, even exciting. But halfway through, reality shows up. Breathing gets harder. Legs tighten. That early surge starts costing you.

Smart runners do not panic.

They settle back into rhythm. They adjust stride. They manage effort. They do not sprint to make up time immediately. They rebalance effort so they can finish strong.

Financially, rebalancing is that moment.

You notice something drifting. Stocks are running hot. Bonds are lagging. Cash feels light. The instinct is either to ignore it or overcorrect. Discipline lives in the middle.

How Often to Review Investments

One of the biggest mistakes athletes make is checking too often.

In training, you do not test race pace every day. You trust the process. You review progress at planned intervals.

Money should work the same way.

Reviewing your investments too frequently creates noise. Daily or weekly checking magnifies emotion. Every fluctuation feels meaningful even when it is not. That leads to reaction, not strategy.

Most long-term plans only require review a few times a year.

Think seasonally.

Preseason. Midseason. Postseason.

Those are natural checkpoints. You look at alignment, not performance alone. Are you still running the right race? Are you pacing correctly? Are fundamentals intact?

Reviewing less often protects discipline. It keeps you focused on execution, not distractions.

What Rebalancing Actually Means

Rebalancing is not about predicting the future.

It is about restoring balance.

Over time, different investments grow at different speeds. Stocks may surge. Bonds may lag. Cash may shrink as you invest. Without adjustment, your portfolio drifts away from your intended risk level.

In track terms, this is pacing drift.

You did not plan to run the first half too fast. It just happened. Rebalancing is easing back into rhythm, not slamming on the brakes.

Financially, rebalancing often means trimming what has grown too large and adding to what has fallen behind. It feels uncomfortable because it asks you to sell winners and buy laggards.

That discomfort is a feature, not a flaw.

Rebalancing Strategies That Actually Work

There is no single perfect method. What matters is consistency.

Some athletes rebalance on a schedule. Once or twice per year, they restore allocations back to target. Simple. Predictable. Effective.

Others rebalance when allocations drift beyond set ranges. If stocks exceed target by a certain percentage, adjustments are made. This method requires awareness but less emotion.

Both encourages discipline.

The mistake is rebalancing reactively. Adjusting because of headlines. Adjusting because of fear. Adjusting because something feels urgent.

In racing terms, that is surging every time someone passes you. It wastes energy and rarely improves outcome.

Rebalancing is planned. Calm. Intentional.

Life Changes and Portfolio Updates

Not all adjustments come from markets.

Life creates changes that matter more than returns.

New job.

Income changes.

Marriage.

Kids.

Injury.

Career transition.

Unexpected opportunity or setback.

These moments change your time horizon, flexibility, and risk capacity.

In track terms, this is switching events or moving up in distance. You do not train the same way for a 400 as you do for a 10K. Pretending nothing changed creates injury.

Financial plans should evolve with life, not resist it.

Rebalancing after life changes is not failure. It is maturity.

You are not quitting the race. You are adjusting strategy for new conditions.

Avoiding Over-Adjustment

Over-adjustment is the silent killer of progress.

Small discomfort triggers action. Minor underperformance sparks major changes. Confidence erodes. Structure collapses.

Athletes do this when they change workouts weekly. Shoes constantly. Diet daily. Nothing compounds.

Financially, over-adjustment looks like:

Constant strategy changes

Chasing recent performance

Selling during stress

Buying during hype

Every adjustment carries cost. Taxes. Fees. Missed recovery. Mental fatigue.

Great racers know when not to adjust.

They accept temporary discomfort. They trust training. They conserve energy for when it matters.

In money, restraint is a skill.

Emotional Discipline During Volatility

Volatility is normal.

Markets move. Prices fluctuate. That movement does not mean something is broken.

In racing terms, this is terrain change. Hills feel harder. Downhills feel fast. You do not abandon form because of elevation.

Emotion turns volatility into mistakes.

Fear tells you to stop.

Greed tells you to sprint.

Comparison tells you you are behind.

None of those voices care about your long-term finish.

Rebalancing exists to remove emotion from adjustment. You are not deciding based on feeling. You are executing a pre-planned response.

That is discipline.

Coach's Perspective

What would your coach say?

"Run your race."

"Stay in rhythm."

"Do not panic."

"Make adjustments, not excuses."

"Finish strong."

Coaches do not want emotional athletes. They want composed competitors who can adjust without losing form.

That is exactly what rebalancing builds financially.

Game Situations and Decision Points

Markets surge.

Do you let risk drift higher or rebalance calmly?

Markets drop.

Do you abandon the plan or restore balance?

Life changes.

Do you ignore it or update your strategy?

Every adjustment is a decision. Discipline decides whether it helps or hurts.

Common Athlete Mistakes and Financial Parallels

Athletes react to competition instead of pace.

Financially, that means chasing returns.

Athletes overcorrect small mistakes.

Financially, that means constant changes.

Athletes ignore changing conditions.

Financially, that means outdated plans.

Awareness plus restraint wins races and builds wealth.

Winning the Long Game

No race is static.

Conditions change. Bodies adapt. Strategy evolves.

The goal is not to avoid adjustments. The goal is to make them intentionally and sparingly.

Rebalancing keeps you aligned with your goals. It protects you from extremes. It preserves energy for the final stretch.

That is how disciplined athletes finish strong financially.

Athlete Takeaways

- Review your plan at scheduled checkpoints, not every day
- Rebalancing restores rhythm, not prediction
- Adjust for life changes, not headlines
- Over-adjustment wastes energy and focus
- Stay composed, trust the plan, finish the race

Chapter 18: The Mental Side of Money

Every runner eventually learns this lesson the hard way.

The race is not lost in your legs first.

It is lost in your head.

Your body can handle more than you think. Your training prepared you for discomfort. What breaks people is panic. Doubt. Comparison. The moment when you stop running your race and start reacting to everything around you.

Money works the same way.

Most financial mistakes are not caused by lack of intelligence. They are caused by fear, pressure, and distraction. The mental side of money is what determines whether good plans survive real-world stress.

If you cannot stay mentally composed, the best financial strategy in the world will not save you.

Opening Story From the Sport

Think about a race where the crowd is loud and the competition is stacked.

You hear footsteps behind you. Someone surges past. Another runner moves wide. The noise grows. Suddenly, everything outside of you feels urgent. You feel pressure to respond immediately. To push harder than planned. To prove something.

Sometimes that surge works.

Most of the time, it costs the race.

The athletes who finish strongest are not the ones who ignore the crowd.

They are the ones who filter it. They know what matters and what does not. They stick to rhythm. They trust preparation.

Financially, the crowd is always loud.

News headlines.

Social media.

Friends talking about wins.

Family opinions.

Market commentary.

The challenge is not hearing the noise. The challenge is staying focused anyway.

Fear, Pressure, and Comparison

Fear shows up when money feels uncertain.

A market drop.

An unexpected bill.

A missed opportunity.

A feeling of being behind.

Pressure shows up when expectations rise.

More income.

More responsibility.

More eyes watching your decisions.

Comparison shows up when you start measuring your race against someone else's.

They bought a house.

They made money on a hot investment.

They seem ahead.

In track terms, fear tightens your stride. Pressure speeds you up too early. Comparison pulls you out of your lane.

None of those improve performance.

Fear makes people freeze.

Pressure makes people force decisions.

Comparison makes people abandon plans.

Money does not reward urgency. It rewards composure.

Crowd Noise and External Expectations

Every athlete understands crowd noise.

Some people feed off it. Others get rattled by it. Either way, it is there whether you want it or not.

Money has crowd noise too.

Parents who worry.

Friends who brag.

Social media posts that highlight wins but hide losses.

Headlines designed to trigger emotion.

The noise is not designed to help you. It is designed to capture attention.

In racing, you do not let the crowd dictate pace. You let your watch, your breathing, and your training do that.

Financially, you need the same filters.

Not every opinion deserves weight.

Not every headline deserves action.

Not every success story applies to you.

External expectations create pressure to act. Discipline creates permission to wait.

Why Perfectionism Hurts Financial Progress

Many athletes carry perfectionism long after competition ends.

It helped you once.

It pushed standards higher.

It demanded excellence.

Financially, perfectionism becomes a problem.

People wait for the perfect budget.

The perfect investment.

The perfect timing.

The perfect plan.

While they wait, nothing happens.

In track, waiting for perfect conditions means never racing. You compete with what you have on the day you have it.

Money requires the same mindset.

Progress beats perfection.

Execution beats planning.

Consistency beats brilliance.

Perfectionism is just fear wearing a cleaner uniform.

Building Systems for Discipline

Discipline does not come from willpower.

It comes from systems.

Athletes know this instinctively. You do not rely on motivation to train. You rely on schedules, habits, and accountability.

Money should work the same way.

Automatic savings.

Scheduled investing.

Clear rules for spending.

Predefined rebalancing plans.

These systems remove emotion from decisions.

You are not deciding in the moment. You are executing a plan made when you were calm.

That is how champions operate.

The more your system handles, the less your emotions interfere.

Staying Focused During Volatility

Volatility is movement.

It is not danger.

It is not failure.

It is not a signal to abandon the plan.

Markets move like terrain. Hills. Turns. Wind. Conditions change constantly.

Runners do not quit when the course gets hard. They adjust effort and keep moving.

Financial volatility tests mental toughness more than intelligence.

Red numbers trigger fear.

Green numbers trigger greed.

Both tempt reaction.

Staying focused means remembering what the race actually is.

This is not a sprint.

This is not a single season.

This is a career-length event.

Short-term movement does not change long-term direction unless you let it.

The Role of Identity After Competition

One of the hardest mental shifts for former athletes is identity.

In sport, effort is visible.

Results are immediate.

Feedback is constant.

Money does not work that way.

Progress is slow.

Wins are quiet.

Feedback is delayed.

Without a uniform or scoreboard, it is easy to feel lost or impatient. That discomfort leads people to seek validation through spending, risk-taking, or comparison.

Strong financial discipline requires redefining identity.

You are no longer proving yourself every weekend.

You are building quietly.

You are stacking invisible wins.

That is harder than competition.

It is also where real success lives.

Coach's Perspective

What would your coach say here?

"Control what you can control."

"Stay in your lane."

"Trust your training."

"Do not let the moment speed you up."

"Finish the race."

Coaches know panic kills performance.

They teach composure under pressure because that is where championships are decided.

Money is no different.

Game Situations and Decision Points

The market drops sharply.

Do you react emotionally or follow the plan?

You hear about someone making fast money.

Do you compare or stay disciplined?

You feel pressure to act.

Do you pause or force a move?

Every one of these moments tests mental strength, not knowledge.

Common Athlete Mistakes and Financial Parallels

Athletes chase competitors instead of pace.

Financially, that is comparison-driven decisions.

Athletes panic under pressure.

Financially, that is emotional selling or buying.

Athletes abandon training when results lag.

Financially, that is quitting consistency too early.

The mind breaks before the body. The same is true with money.

Winning the Long Game

Financial success is not about being fearless.

It is about being composed.

You will feel fear.

You will feel pressure.

You will hear noise.

The athletes who win long-term are the ones who acknowledge those feelings without obeying them.

They trust systems.

They trust time.

They trust discipline.

That is how races are won.

That is how wealth is built.

Athlete Takeaways

- Stay in your lane and run your plan
- Crowd noise is real, but it is not instruction
- Systems beat motivation every time
- Volatility tests mindset, not intelligence
- Composure under pressure wins the long race

Part V: The Long Season and Life Beyond Competition

Every track athlete understands seasons.

There is the competitive season when everything revolves around performance. There is the offseason when the work is quieter, less visible, but just as important. And then there is the long arc of development that stretches far beyond any single meet, year, or PR.

Money follows the same rhythm.

Early on, financial decisions feel urgent. Income changes. Careers shift. Big choices show up fast. Over time, the focus changes from speed to sustainability. From chasing outcomes to protecting progress. From short races to a long season that includes family, career transitions, health, and purpose.

This part of the book is about that long season.

It is about managing money when the uniform comes off and there is no finish line tape waiting for you. It is about planning for decades, not quarters. It is about making decisions that still hold up when life changes, priorities shift, and responsibilities grow.

You will not always feel fast.

You will not always feel certain.

You will not always feel ahead.

But you can stay prepared.

The athletes who thrive after competition are not the ones who sprint hardest early. They are the ones who pace themselves, adapt when conditions change, and keep showing up with discipline long after the spotlight fades.

This section focuses on taxes, retirement, housing, career decisions, estate planning, and family conversations. These are not glamorous topics, but they are decisive ones. They determine whether the work you put in during your competitive years compounds into freedom or fades into stress.

The long season rewards patience.

Life beyond competition rewards structure.

Winning here is about staying healthy, flexible, and intentional.

You are no longer racing others.

You are building a life.

And just like track, how you manage the later miles determines how strong you finish.

Chapter 19: Taxes and Where You Place Your Effort

Every track athlete learns this lesson the hard way.

You can be in incredible shape, but if you waste energy in the wrong places, the race still falls apart. Going out too fast. Fighting the wind instead of drafting. Overstriding on the curve. None of those mistakes look dramatic in isolation, but they compound quickly. By the final laps, you are exhausted and confused about where it went wrong.

Taxes work the same way.

Most athletes do not lose money because they are lazy or careless. They lose money because they place effort in the wrong places. They focus on returns without thinking about taxes. They chase income without understanding how it is taxed. They work hard, but the structure quietly drains performance.

Taxes are not just a once-a-year event. They are part of every financial stride you take. Where you place your money matters just as much as how hard that money works.

This chapter is about efficiency. Not avoiding taxes illegally. Not gaming the system. Simply understanding where effort belongs so you are not running uphill when you do not have to.

Opening Story From Track

Think about a long race, maybe the 5K or 10K.

You feel strong early. Your splits look good. But somewhere around the middle, you realize something is off. Your breathing is labored. Your legs feel heavier than they should. You are still moving, but the effort-to-result ratio is terrible.

Later, when you look back, the problem is obvious. You fought the wind alone instead of tucking in. You surged at the wrong time. You wasted energy when patience would have carried you farther.

Taxes create the same invisible drag.

You can earn, invest, and save, but if your money is placed in the wrong accounts, taxes quietly sap momentum year after year. You may not notice it early. Over decades, it changes everything.

Taxable vs Tax-Advantaged Accounts

Not all money is treated the same by the tax system.

Taxable accounts are exactly what they sound like. Interest, dividends, and capital gains are taxed along the way. Brokerage accounts, savings accounts, and some investment accounts fall into this category.

Tax-advantaged accounts offer special treatment. They are designed to encourage long-term behavior. Retirement accounts, health savings accounts, and education-focused accounts reward patience with lower taxes or no taxes at all.

In track terms, this is lane choice.

Some lanes have headwinds. Others are smoother and protected. You can still run fast in a bad lane, but it takes more effort to get the same result.

Many athletes focus only on what they invest in and ignore where they invest it. That is like obsessing over shoes while ignoring the surface you are running on.

Tax-Deferred vs Tax-Free Growth

This distinction matters more than most people realize.

Tax-deferred growth means you postpone taxes. You do not avoid them. Traditional retirement accounts work this way. You may get a tax break today, but you pay taxes later when you withdraw.

Tax-free growth means qualified withdrawals are not taxed at all. Roth-style accounts work this way. You pay taxes upfront, but future growth is yours to keep.

In track terms, tax-deferred is pacing later discomfort. Tax-free is doing harder work earlier so the finish is cleaner.

Neither is automatically better. The right choice depends on income level, career stage, and future expectations.

Athletes early in their careers often benefit from tax-free growth because income may rise later. Athletes in peak earning years may value deferral to manage current tax pressure.

The mistake is not choosing wrong. The mistake is not choosing intentionally.

Asset Location Basics

Asset allocation gets a lot of attention. Stocks versus bonds. Growth versus value. Domestic versus international.

Asset location gets almost none.

Asset location is about placing the right investments in the right accounts. Some investments generate more taxable income than others. Some benefit more from tax protection.

In track terms, this is assigning the right runner to the right leg of a relay.

High-income, tax-inefficient investments often belong in tax-advantaged accounts. More tax-efficient investments can live in taxable accounts with less drag.

When asset location is ignored, you are forcing every runner to fight the hardest section of the course. The team still runs, but performance suffers.

Small decisions here compound for decades.

How Taxes Quietly Change Returns

Taxes are rarely felt all at once.

They show up as slightly lower balances. Slightly slower growth. Slightly less flexibility. Over time, those small differences separate outcomes dramatically.

In track terms, this is cumulative fatigue.

One inefficient stride does not ruin a race. Thousands of them do.

Many athletes chase higher returns while ignoring taxes. That is like sprinting uphill while ignoring pacing. You may feel aggressive, but efficiency matters more than intensity.

Common Tax Mistakes Athletes Make

Mistake One: Ignoring Taxes Until April

Taxes are treated as an annual surprise instead of a year-round factor. Decisions are made without considering consequences.

Mistake Two: Confusing Income With Take-Home Pay

Gross income feels big. Net income is what actually matters. Taxes change lifestyle math quickly.

Mistake Three: Using the Wrong Accounts

Saving in taxable accounts while ignoring tax-advantaged options wastes opportunity.

Mistake Four: Overtrading Investments

Frequent buying and selling creates unnecessary tax friction. Activity feels productive. It is often harmful.

Mistake Five: Assuming Taxes Will Be Lower Later

Future tax rates are unknown. Blind assumptions lead to poor positioning.

In track terms, these are unforced errors. No opponent caused them. They came from lack of awareness.

Coach's Perspective

A coach would not overcomplicate this.

Control what you can control.

Be efficient.

Do not waste energy.

Run your race smart.

They would not expect perfection. They would expect awareness.

Taxes are part of the course. Ignoring them does not make you tough. It makes you inefficient.

Game Situations and Decision Points

You get a raise. Do you adjust savings and account types, or just increase spending?

You open a new investment account. Do you consider taxes, or just returns?

You feel behind. Do you chase aggressive moves, or tighten efficiency?

Each decision either reduces drag or increases it.

Common Athlete Mistakes and Financial Parallels

Athletes sprint too early.

Financially, that looks like ignoring taxes for short-term gains.

Athletes fight conditions instead of adapting.

Financially, that looks like using the wrong accounts.

Athletes confuse effort with progress.

Financially, that looks like overactivity.

The same discipline that wins races builds wealth.

Winning the Long Game

Taxes are not the enemy. They are part of the environment.

Smart athletes learn to work with conditions, not against them. They draft when possible. They surge when it matters. They conserve energy for the finish.

Placing your money in the right accounts does not guarantee success. It improves odds. It increases efficiency. It protects progress.

Over decades, that matters more than chasing fast times.

Athlete Takeaways

- Pick the right lane. Where money lives matters as much as how hard it works.
- Pace the tax bill. Deferred and tax-free growth serve different parts of the race.
- Efficiency beats effort. Reduce drag before chasing speed.
- Avoid unforced errors. Taxes punish impatience and overactivity.
- Run smart miles now so the finish is strong later.

Chapter 20: Retirement Accounts and Financial Independence

Every runner eventually learns this lesson the hard way.

You cannot sprint the entire race.

Even the fastest athletes in the world pace themselves. They understand when to settle in, when to surge, and when to conserve energy so they still have something left at the finish. The runners who fail are not the ones who lack talent. They are the ones who spend everything too early and have nothing left when it matters most.

Retirement planning works the same way.

Financial independence is not about quitting work at a specific age or hitting some flashy number. It is about building enough strength, endurance, and systems so you are not forced to keep running when your body, priorities, or life circumstances change.

Retirement accounts are not exciting. They are not fast. They are not glamorous.

They are distance training.

Opening Story From Track

Think about a long-distance season.

Early workouts are not about speed. They are about base mileage. Aerobic capacity. Teaching your body how to handle volume without breaking down. The work feels boring compared to intervals or race pace reps, but it is what allows you to perform later.

Retirement accounts play that exact role in your financial life.

They are designed for the long haul. You do not feel immediate payoff. There are rules, limits, and restrictions. That is intentional. These accounts exist to protect you from burning out financially before the race is over.

The athletes who commit to base training early do not panic later. The same is true with retirement planning.

Employer Plans and Pensions

For many athletes and former athletes, the first real exposure to retirement saving comes through an employer plan.

401(k). 403(b). 457. TSP.

These are employer-sponsored retirement accounts designed to make saving automatic.

In track terms, this is organized team training. The structure is built in. You show up. The reps happen whether you feel motivated or not.

Key advantages of employer plans:

- Contributions come directly from your paycheck
- Some employers offer matching contributions
- Money grows tax-advantaged
- Automation removes decision fatigue

Employer match is especially important. A match is free distance covered. Leaving it unused is like skipping a lap you are already credited for.

Pensions, while less common today, function differently. They promise a future income stream based on years of service and earnings. In track terms, a pension is like a guaranteed pace car late in the race. You still need other training, but it provides stability.

The mistake athletes make is treating employer plans as optional. These plans are foundational mileage. You do not skip them because they feel slow.

Traditional and Roth IRAs

IRAs give you more individual control.

Traditional IRA:

- Contributions may reduce current taxes
- Money grows tax-deferred
- Withdrawals are taxed later

Roth IRA:

- Contributions are made with after-tax money
- Money grows tax-free
- Qualified withdrawals are tax-free

In track terms, this is choosing how you distribute effort.

Traditional accounts reduce effort now and push it later.

Roth accounts increase effort now so the finish is cleaner.

Neither is universally better. The right choice depends on:

- Current income
- Expected future income
- Career stage
- Tax environment
- Flexibility needs

Early-career athletes often benefit from Roth contributions because income is lower and time is long. Later-career athletes may value the tax deferral of traditional accounts.

The key is not perfection. The key is consistent contribution.

Contribution Rules and Limits

Retirement accounts come with rules. That is not a flaw. That is protection.

Contribution limits prevent you from over-relying on one tool. Income limits determine eligibility. Penalties discourage early withdrawals.

In track terms, these are training boundaries. They prevent overtraining and injury.

You cannot shortcut retirement saving by dumping everything in at the last minute. The system rewards consistency over time.

Athletes who try to "make it up later" financially often discover the same truth runners do. Missed mileage is hard to replace.

Withdrawal Rules and Access

One of the biggest sources of confusion is access.

Retirement accounts are not designed for short-term needs. Pulling money out early often triggers taxes and penalties. That friction is intentional.

In track terms, this is race-day discipline. You do not sprint early just because you feel good. The structure forces patience.

That said, some flexibility exists:

- Roth contributions can often be accessed before earnings
- Certain hardship withdrawals are allowed
- Loan options exist in some employer plans

These should be emergency exits, not strategy.

If you regularly need to access retirement money, the problem is not the account. The problem is missing base training elsewhere, like savings or cash flow management.

Retirement Income Basics

Saving for retirement is only half the equation.

The goal is income.

Retirement income can come from:

- Withdrawals from retirement accounts
- Employer pensions
- Social Security
- Investment income
- Part-time work or consulting

In track terms, this is race execution. Training matters, but how you run the race determines the outcome.

Financial independence means your income sources are diversified and flexible. You are not relying on one fragile system.

The mistake many athletes make is focusing only on the account balance. Balance matters, but income sustainability matters more.

You are not trying to hit a number. You are trying to control pace for the rest of your life.

Why Athletes Struggle With Long-Term Planning

Athletes are trained to focus on the next race, the next season, the next performance.

Retirement feels abstract. Far away. Slow.

That mindset works in sport. It backfires financially.

The earlier you build retirement systems, the less pressure you feel later. Small, consistent contributions early often outperform aggressive saving late.

In track terms, this is starting base training before competition season. You are not chasing fitness. You are building it.

Coach's Perspective

A coach would not sugarcoat this.

You cannot fake endurance.

Mileage matters.

Reps matter.

Do not cheat the work.

Finish strong.

They would remind you that long-term success is built quietly, long before anyone is watching.

Retirement accounts are quiet work. That is why they work.

Game Situations and Decision Points

Your employer offers a match. Do you take it, or leave free distance on the track?

You qualify for a Roth IRA. Do you use it, or wait for "later"?

You want to pause contributions for lifestyle reasons. Do you understand what that costs over time?

Each decision affects how hard the later miles will feel.

Common Athlete Mistakes and Financial Parallels

Athletes delay base training.

Financially, that shows up as delayed retirement saving.

Athletes overvalue speed.

Financially, that shows up as short-term focus.

Athletes assume they can catch up later.

Financially, that leads to stress and forced decisions.

Distance rewards patience.

Winning the Long Game

Financial independence is not about escaping work. It is about choice.

Choice to slow down.

Choice to pivot.

Choice to rest.

Choice to keep running because you want to, not because you have to.

Retirement accounts are not exciting because they are not meant to be. They are meant to carry you across the finish line with strength left in your legs.

Athlete Takeaways

- Retirement accounts are distance training, not sprint work
- Employer matches are free miles. Never skip them
- Roth and traditional accounts shift effort between now and later
- Consistent contributions beat late aggression
- Train for the finish, not just the first lap

Chapter 21: Housing and Major Financial Decisions

Every runner remembers the first time a race went wrong because of one bad decision.

Maybe you went out too fast because the pack surged. Maybe you chased someone who was not in your race. Maybe you ignored how you felt and committed to a move you could not sustain. The mistake was not effort. The mistake was timing and judgment.

Housing and major purchases work the same way.

Most financial damage does not come from daily spending. It comes from a handful of large decisions made at the wrong time, under the wrong assumptions, or for the wrong reasons. Where you live. What you drive. How you finance big purchases. These choices shape cash flow, flexibility, stress levels, and long-term options.

This chapter is about pacing. Not fear. Not avoiding commitment forever. Knowing when to commit and when to stay light on your feet so you do not lock yourself into a race you cannot finish strong.

Opening Story From Track

Think about a championship meet.

You have trained for months. You feel ready. Then, just before the race, someone else makes a big move early. The crowd reacts. Adrenaline spikes. Everything in you wants to respond immediately.

Great runners pause.

They ask one question before reacting: *Does this move fit my race plan?*

Housing and major purchases create that same moment. Friends buy houses. Teammates upgrade cars. Social media shows milestones that feel like progress. The pressure is subtle but real.

The question is never "Can I do this?"

The question is "Does this fit my plan, my timing, and my long-term race?"

Renting vs Buying

Renting and buying are not moral decisions. One is not winning. The other is not losing.

Renting buys flexibility.

Buying commits you to a course.

In track terms, renting is staying in the pack with room to adjust. Buying is committing to a long surge and holding it.

Renting makes sense when:

- Income is unstable or early in your career
- You may relocate for work or opportunity
- You value simplicity and flexibility
- You are still building savings and margin

Buying makes sense when:

- Income is stable and predictable
- You plan to stay in one location for years
- You have adequate savings beyond the purchase
- You are ready for responsibility and variability

The biggest mistake athletes make is treating buying a home like a finish line. It is not. It is a checkpoint. And it comes with ongoing effort.

Buying before you are ready is like committing to a pace you cannot hold.

You might survive the first miles. The later ones get ugly.

The Hidden Costs of Homeownership

Most people focus on the obvious numbers.

Purchase price. Monthly payment. Interest rate.

The real costs show up quietly.

Maintenance. Repairs. Property taxes. Insurance. Utilities. Unexpected expenses. Reduced mobility.

In track terms, this is running with added weight you did not account for. The pace that felt manageable at first slowly drains you.

Homeownership can be a strong long-term move. It becomes a financial anchor when purchased without margin.

If one repair, one job change, or one income disruption creates panic, the timing was wrong.

Mortgages and Down Payments

A mortgage is leverage. It allows you to control a large asset with borrowed money.

Leverage amplifies outcomes. It helps when things go well. It hurts when they do not.

In track terms, leverage is drafting. It can save energy, but only if conditions remain stable.

Down payments are about margin, not just approval. A smaller down payment may get you into a house faster, but it leaves less buffer. A larger down payment reduces monthly stress and increases flexibility.

The best mortgage is not the biggest one you qualify for. It is the one you can comfortably carry through bad conditions.

Weather changes. Injuries happen. Careers shift.

Strong runners plan for bad days, not just perfect ones.

Cars, Leases, and Financing Traps

Cars are one of the fastest ways athletes sabotage cash flow.

They are emotional purchases. They are visible. They feel like progress. They depreciate.

In track terms, this is sprinting to look strong in the first lap and paying for it later.

Financing traps show up in a few forms:

- Stretching loan terms to lower payments
- Leasing without understanding total cost
- Buying more car than income can comfortably support
- Upgrading frequently because payments feel manageable

Payments that "feel fine" still steal future flexibility. Every fixed payment narrows your options.

Transportation should support your life, not quietly control it.

A reliable, reasonable vehicle that keeps cash flow clean often wins the long race over flashy upgrades.

Why Big Purchases Feel Harder Than They Look

Large financial decisions are rarely about math alone.

They involve identity. Status. Validation. Fear of being behind.

Athletes are especially vulnerable because structure disappears after sport. Without scoreboards and rankings, milestones become substitutes for progress.

House. Car. Lifestyle.

These are not bad goals. They become dangerous when used as proof of success instead of tools that support it.

In track terms, this is confusing pace with position. Being ahead early does not mean you are winning.

Planning Major Purchases Like a Race Strategy

Major purchases deserve the same planning you gave competition.

You would never show up to a race without knowing:

- Distance
- Conditions
- Competition
- Your fitness
- Your strategy

Apply the same discipline.

Before a major purchase, ask:

- How does this affect monthly cash flow?
- How does it affect flexibility if income changes?
- What am I giving up to afford this?
- Am I making this decision to move forward, or to keep up?

If the answers feel rushed or emotional, slow down.

Great runners know when to wait.

Coach's Perspective

A coach would say it clearly.

Run your race.

Do not chase the pack.

Protect your energy.

Finish strong.

They would remind you that early confidence means nothing if you cannot close.

Major purchases are not about proving anything. They are about sustaining performance over time.

Game Situations and Decision Points

You qualify for a larger mortgage. Do you take it, or choose margin?

Your friends upgrade cars. Do you follow, or stick to your plan?

You feel behind. Do you rush a purchase, or strengthen your base first?

Each decision either preserves flexibility or trades it away.

Common Athlete Mistakes and Financial Parallels

Athletes chase early position.

Financially, that shows up as premature buying.

Athletes ignore conditions.

Financially, that shows up as underestimating risk.

Athletes mistake confidence for readiness.

Financially, that leads to overcommitment.

The same discipline that wins races prevents regret.

Winning the Long Game

Housing and major purchases are not sprints. They are long efforts that affect every mile that follows.

You do not need to avoid commitment forever. You need to commit at the right time, with the right margin, for the right reasons.

Strong runners are patient. They trust preparation. They make moves when they know they can hold them.

Money rewards the same mindset.

Athlete Takeaways

- Run your race. Timing matters more than appearances.
- Margin is strength. Big commitments need breathing room.
- Payments limit flexibility. Choose them carefully.
- Major purchases should support the plan, not replace it.

- Finish strong beats starting fast every time.

Chapter 22: Your Career Is Your Longest Event

Track athletes understand something most people miss.

The race you win today does not matter if you cannot sustain the season.

You can peak too early.

You can burn out.

You can train perfectly for one event and quietly sabotage the long-term outcome.

Your career works the same way.

It is not a sprint.

It is not one contract, one promotion, or one good year.

It is the longest event you will ever run, and every decision you make affects your pace, recovery, and longevity.

Most financial success is not driven by investments first. It is driven by income stability, growth, and decision-making across a career. If you get this part wrong, everything else becomes harder. If you get it right, the rest of the plan becomes easier to execute.

Opening Story From Track

Think about a multi-year training cycle.

You do not train the same way at 18 as you do at 28. You do not race the same schedule every season. You adapt based on health, performance, competition, and opportunity.

Athletes who last understand that training is not just about effort. It is about planning, progression, and recovery.

Your career is no different.

You are training your earning ability, your skills, your network, and your reputation over decades. One bad decision will not ruin you. A pattern of poor decisions will.

This is not about finding the perfect job. It is about building a career that supports your life long after competition ends.

Salary vs Total Compensation

Most athletes fixate on salary.

Salary is important, but it is not the full picture.

Total compensation includes:

- Base pay
- Bonuses
- Overtime or commissions
- Retirement contributions
- Health insurance
- Disability coverage
- Paid time off
- Education benefits
- Equity or profit sharing

In track terms, salary is your race result. Total compensation is the entire training environment.

Two jobs with the same salary can produce wildly different outcomes over time depending on benefits, stability, and growth opportunities.

A slightly lower salary with strong benefits and career development can outperform a higher salary with no support.

Do not judge offers by one number. Judge them by how they support consistency, recovery, and long-term progress.

Benefits Are Part of Your Training Program

Athletes understand the value of support staff.

Trainers.

Physical therapists.

Nutrition.

Facilities.

Benefits play the same role in your career.

Health insurance protects availability.

Retirement plans support long-term independence.

Paid time off prevents burnout.

Disability insurance protects income when things go wrong.

Ignoring benefits is like training without access to rehab. You may be fine for a while. When something breaks, the cost is massive.

Benefits rarely feel exciting. They quietly determine whether you can keep showing up.

Job Changes and Career Transitions

Athletes change events, coaches, and programs when it makes sense.

Careers require the same adaptability.

Job changes are not failures. They are adjustments.

Common reasons to change roles include:

- Skill growth
- Better mentorship
- Improved compensation structure
- Healthier culture
- Better alignment with long-term goals

The mistake is changing jobs reactively instead of intentionally.

In track terms, this is chasing races without a training plan. You might get lucky. You might also stall development.

Before changing roles, ask:

- What am I running toward, not just away from?
- Does this improve long-term earning power?
- Does this align with my life outside work?

Smart transitions improve pace without burning energy.

Understanding Risk in Career Decisions

Career risk is different from investment risk.

Investment risk shows up on statements.

Career risk shows up slowly.

Unstable income.

No benefits.

Limited growth.

Burnout.

Athletes often underestimate career risk because they are comfortable competing under pressure. That confidence can lead to ignoring warning signs.

In track terms, this is racing while injured because you feel tough enough to handle it. It works until it does not.

Stability matters.

Growth matters.

Recovery matters.

A career that destroys your health or limits your future options is not a win, even if it looks impressive today.

Negotiation Basics

Negotiation intimidates many former athletes.

That is ironic, because athletes negotiate constantly:

- Playing time
- Roles
- Training expectations
- Competitive opportunities

Negotiation is not confrontation. It is communication.

At its core, negotiation is about understanding value.

Your value comes from:

- Skills
- Experience
- Reliability
- Results
- Scarcity

In track terms, this is knowing your event and knowing your strengths. You do not ask to run a race you are not prepared for. You also do not undersell what you bring.

Negotiation basics:

- Be informed
- Be respectful
- Be clear
- Be willing to walk away

You do not need to win every negotiation. You need to avoid losing leverage by staying silent.

Side Income and Entrepreneurship

Many athletes are drawn to side income.

That makes sense. You are used to stacking effort. You see opportunity everywhere.

Side income can be powerful when:

- Core income is stable
- Time and energy are managed
- Risk is understood
- Expectations are realistic

Side income becomes dangerous when:

- It replaces rest
- It creates distraction
- It adds stress
- It becomes speculative

In track terms, this is adding extra workouts. Extra training helps when programmed correctly. It leads to injury when forced.

Entrepreneurship is not a shortcut. It is a different race with different demands.

If you pursue side income, treat it like training:

- Start small
- Track results
- Adjust based on feedback
- Protect recovery

Why Athletes Struggle After Sports

Structure disappears.

Feedback becomes vague.

Progress feels unclear.

In track, improvement is measured in times and places. Careers rarely give you that clarity.

That lack of feedback causes athletes to:

- Chase money instead of growth
- Prioritize comfort over development
- Stay in bad situations too long
- Jump too quickly without direction

The solution is building your own scoreboard.

Define success beyond salary.

Track skill growth.

Measure stability.

Protect health.

Coach's Perspective

A coach would not sugarcoat it.

Train for the season, not the workout.

Recover so you can compete again.

Do not sacrifice the future for one race.

Be patient.

Stack good days.

Your career is about durability, not just performance.

Game Situations and Decision Points

You get a job offer with higher pay but no benefits. Do you evaluate total compensation or chase salary?

You feel bored in your role. Do you develop skills or jump without a plan?

You want side income. Do you assess energy and risk or assume you can handle everything?

Same principles. Different arena.

Common Athlete Mistakes and Financial Parallels

Athletes chase fast times.

Financially, that means chasing salary without structure.

Athletes ignore recovery.

Financially, that means burnout and poor decisions.

Athletes underestimate long seasons.

Financially, that means short-term thinking.

Winning the Long Game

Your career funds your life.

It supports saving.

It enables investing.

It provides flexibility.

It protects independence.

Treat it like the longest event you will ever run.

Pace matters.

Structure matters.

Recovery matters.

You do not need to win every year.

You need to keep running strong.

Athlete Takeaways

- Salary is one split. Total compensation is the full race
- Benefits protect availability and longevity
- Job changes should improve long-term pace, not just comfort
- Negotiation is communication, not confrontation
- Your career is your longest event. Train for it accordingly

Chapter 23: Estate Planning Basics Everyone Needs

Track athletes understand preparation in a way most people never will.

You do not show up to a meet hoping nothing goes wrong. You plan for weather. You plan for rounds. You plan for travel delays, tight schedules, and worst-case scenarios. Preparation is not pessimism. It is professionalism.

Estate planning works the same way.

It is not about expecting something bad to happen. It is about making sure that if life changes suddenly, your people are protected, your wishes are honored, and your hard work is not undone by confusion or legal messes.

Most people avoid estate planning because it feels uncomfortable, distant, or unnecessary. Former athletes avoid it because it feels like something you deal with "later." That mindset creates problems that show up at the worst possible time.

Estate planning is not about death.

It is about control.

It is about clarity.

It is about protecting the race you already ran.

Opening Story From Track

Every experienced runner knows the difference between preparation and panic.

If you forget your spikes, your warm-ups, or your race plan, everything feels rushed. Stress rises. Focus drops. Performance suffers. Even if you are fit, poor preparation can ruin the day.

Estate planning is the same.

When there is no plan, families scramble. Decisions are rushed. Emotions are high. Legal processes take over. The people you care about are left guessing instead of guided.

A simple plan prevents chaos. Just like a race plan prevents panic.

Why Estate Planning Matters Earlier Than You Think

Many people believe estate planning is only for:

- Older adults
- Wealthy families
- People with complex assets

That belief is wrong.

Estate planning matters as soon as you have:

- Income
- Savings
- Retirement accounts
- Dependents
- Strong opinions about your health care or finances

Athletes often have unique risk profiles. Injuries happen. Careers change. Income can be unpredictable. Estate planning is not optional when life moves fast.

In track terms, this is having an emergency race plan even when you expect a clean race.

Wills: The Starting Point

A will is the foundation.

It answers basic questions:

- Who receives your assets?
- Who is responsible for carrying out your wishes?
- Who becomes guardian of minor children?

Without a will, the state decides.

That means laws, not relationships, control outcomes. That rarely aligns with what you would choose.

In track terms, a will is your starting blocks. Without them, the race still happens, but you are at a disadvantage before the gun even fires.

A will does not avoid all legal processes, but it provides direction and authority when it matters most.

Trusts: When Control and Efficiency Matter

Trusts are often misunderstood.

People hear "trust" and assume complexity or wealth. In reality, trusts are tools for control, privacy, and efficiency.

Trusts can:

- Avoid probate
- Control how and when assets are distributed
- Protect beneficiaries from poor decisions
- Provide structure for minors or dependents

In track terms, a trust is like pacing technology. It keeps things steady, intentional, and controlled even when conditions change.

Not everyone needs a trust immediately. Some people benefit greatly from one. The key is understanding when structure adds value.

Beneficiaries: The Most Common Mistake

Beneficiary designations override wills.

That means retirement accounts, life insurance policies, and many investment accounts pass directly to named beneficiaries, regardless of what your will says.

This is where mistakes happen.

Common errors include:

- Forgetting to update beneficiaries
- Naming minors without structure
- Leaving blank or outdated designations
- Assuming a will controls everything

In track terms, this is assuming your relay exchange will work without practicing it. It looks fine on paper. It fails under pressure.

Beneficiary reviews should happen:

- After marriage or divorce
- After children are born
- After major financial changes
- Periodically, even without changes

This is one of the highest-impact, lowest-effort planning steps you can take.

Account Titling: Ownership Matters

How accounts are titled determines what happens when something goes wrong.

Individual accounts, joint accounts, and trust-owned accounts all behave differently.

Improper titling can:

- Delay access to funds
- Create unintended ownership
- Expose assets to unnecessary risk
- Override estate intentions

In track terms, this is lane assignment. The same athlete in the wrong lane faces a very different race.

Titling should match intent. Intent without proper setup leads to confusion.

Powers of Attorney: Control When You Cannot Act

A power of attorney allows someone you trust to make financial or legal decisions if you cannot.

This is not about death.

This is about incapacity.

Accidents, illness, or temporary inability can happen at any age.

Without a power of attorney:

- Bills may go unpaid
- Accounts may be inaccessible
- Legal intervention may be required

In track terms, this is having a backup coach who knows the plan if you cannot make adjustments yourself.

This document keeps life moving when you cannot.

Healthcare Directives: Your Voice When You Cannot Speak

Healthcare directives outline your wishes for medical care and designate someone to make decisions if you cannot.

This includes:

- Treatment preferences
- End-of-life care choices
- Medical decision authority

Athletes are used to trusting medical professionals, but those professionals need guidance.

Without directives, families guess.

Guessing creates conflict.

Conflict creates regret.

In track terms, this is knowing when to push through discomfort and when to stop. You decide ahead of time, not in the middle of chaos.

Why Athletes Avoid Estate Planning

It feels uncomfortable.

It feels premature.

It feels emotional.

It feels like admitting vulnerability.

Athletes are trained to push through discomfort, not sit with it.

But estate planning is not weakness. It is responsibility.

Strong competitors protect their people.

Coach's Perspective

A coach would be direct.

Plan before the race.

Protect your teammates.

Handle your business.

Do not leave things unfinished.

Control what you can control.

Estate planning is not about fear. It is about leadership.

Game Situations and Decision Points

You have retirement accounts but no beneficiaries. Do you update them now or assume it will be fine?

You have children but no will. Do you trust the system or define your wishes?

You have strong opinions about medical care. Do you document them or hope others guess correctly?

Preparation always beats reaction.

Common Athlete Mistakes and Financial Parallels

Athletes avoid uncomfortable prep.

Financially, that means avoiding estate planning.

Athletes assume they have time.

Financially, that leads to rushed decisions later.

Athletes rely on toughness instead of structure.

Financially, that leads to chaos under pressure.

Winning the Long Game

Estate planning protects more than assets.

It protects people.

It protects dignity.

It protects clarity.

It protects the work you already did.

You trained too hard to let confusion undo it.

This is part of finishing strong.

Athlete Takeaways

- A will sets the starting blocks for your wishes
- Beneficiaries matter more than most people realize
- Powers of attorney protect control when you cannot act
- Healthcare directives give you a voice under pressure
- Preparation off the track protects everything you built

Chapter 24: Talking About Money With Family

Track athletes learn early that success is rarely solo.

Even in individual events, nothing happens in isolation. Coaches guide you. Teammates train alongside you. Family supports travel, schedules, and sacrifices. Your performance may be individual, but your environment always matters.

Money works the same way.

No matter how disciplined you are, your financial life intersects with family. Parents. Partners. Kids. Siblings. Aging relatives. Expectations, assumptions, and emotions show up whether you invite them or not. Avoiding money conversations does not protect relationships. It usually strains them.

Learning how to talk about money with family is not about winning arguments. It is about clarity, alignment, and boundaries so you can keep running your race without unnecessary drag.

Opening Story From Track

Every runner remembers their first relay exchange.

You may have been fast. Your teammate may have been fast. But if the handoff was sloppy, the result suffered. Awkward timing. Hesitation. Dropped baton. Everyone leaves frustrated, even though the talent was there.

Family money conversations are baton exchanges.

When expectations are unclear, timing is off, or assumptions go unspoken, problems happen. Not because people are bad, but because communication is missing.

Clean exchanges require practice.

Why Money Is Hard to Talk About With Family

Money carries emotion.

It represents:

- Security
- Sacrifice
- Control
- Fear
- Identity
- Love
- Power

Athletes are comfortable with hard physical conversations. Money conversations are different. They feel personal, loaded, and risky. Families often avoid them until pressure forces the issue.

Avoidance creates silence.

Silence creates assumptions.

Assumptions create resentment.

Talking early prevents blowups later.

Teaching Kids About Money: Starting the Training Early

Track athletes understand that habits form early.

You do not teach form after years of bad mechanics. You teach it before bad habits lock in. Money works the same way with kids.

Teaching kids about money is not about numbers. It is about behavior.

Key lessons include:

- Money is finite
- Choices have tradeoffs
- Saving is normal
- Delayed gratification matters
- Work connects to reward

Age-appropriate exposure matters more than perfection.

Let kids:

- See budgeting decisions
- Save for things they want
- Make small mistakes safely
- Understand needs versus wants

In track terms, this is teaching fundamentals before adding speed.

You are not raising accountants. You are raising disciplined decision-makers.

College Students and Young Adults: Letting Them Run Their Own Race

This stage is tricky.

Young adults want independence.

Parents want protection.

Money becomes the battleground.

College, early careers, and first paychecks introduce real financial decisions:

- Student loans
- Credit cards
- Rent

- Budgeting
- Insurance
- Income volatility

The goal is not control. The goal is coaching.

Helpful approaches:

- Explain consequences instead of issuing commands
- Share experiences, including mistakes
- Encourage systems, not micromanagement
- Let them feel manageable discomfort

In track terms, this is moving from constant instruction to race-day autonomy. You still coach. You just do not run the race for them.

Support without enabling.

Guide without controlling.

Aging Parents and Caregiving: The Reverse Transition

This is one of the hardest shifts.

Parents who once supported you may now need support themselves. Health changes. Income shifts. Cognitive decline. Long-term care decisions.

Many families avoid these conversations until a crisis hits.

That creates:

- Emotional stress
- Financial confusion
- Family conflict
- Rushed decisions

Topics that matter include:

- Where accounts are held

- Who has decision authority
- Healthcare wishes
- Housing preferences
- Care expectations

These conversations are uncomfortable, but they are acts of respect.

In track terms, this is adjusting strategy mid-season when conditions change. Ignoring reality does not preserve dignity. Planning does.

Family Expectations: The Unspoken Pressure

Every family has expectations.

Some are stated.

Most are not.

Examples include:

- Financial support assumptions
- Inheritance expectations
- Lifestyle comparisons
- Cultural obligations
- Guilt-driven decisions

Athletes are used to expectations on performance. Family expectations around money are quieter but just as powerful.

If you do not define boundaries, they get defined for you.

Boundaries are not rejection.

They are clarity.

Clear boundaries allow you to help intentionally instead of resentfully.

Setting Boundaries Without Burning Bridges

Boundaries are not ultimatums.

They are guidelines for how you operate.

Healthy boundaries include:

- What you can help with
- What you cannot help with
- What support looks like
- What support does not look like

Boundaries require repetition. People test them. That does not mean you are wrong.

In track terms, boundaries are lane discipline. Staying in your lane keeps the race clean.

How to Start the Conversation

You do not need a perfect script.

You need honesty and calm.

Good openings include:

- "I want us aligned so there are no surprises."
- "I want to plan before things get stressful."
- "This is uncomfortable, but important."
- "I care about this relationship."

Avoid:

- Blame
- Financial jargon
- Emotional ambushes
- Waiting until conflict forces the issue

Timing matters. Calm moments beat crisis conversations.

Coach's Perspective

A coach would keep it simple.

Communicate early.

Respect the team.

Set expectations.

Protect focus.

Do not let distractions ruin preparation.

Money conversations are part of preparation.

Game Situations and Decision Points

Your parents assume you will help financially. Do you clarify expectations now or let resentment build?

Your adult child struggles with money. Do you bail them out or teach them to adjust?

A family member asks for support that threatens your stability. Do you say yes out of guilt or respond with boundaries?

Just like racing, decisions made under pressure are rarely optimal.

Common Athlete Mistakes and Financial Parallels

Athletes avoid uncomfortable conversations.

Financially, that leads to assumptions.

Athletes try to carry the team alone.

Financially, that leads to burnout.

Athletes ignore communication.

Financially, that leads to conflict.

Winning the Long Game

Healthy money conversations strengthen relationships.

They reduce stress.

They prevent misunderstandings.

They protect respect.

They allow everyone to run their own race.

You cannot control how others respond. You can control clarity, honesty, and discipline.

That is how you finish strong without dragging unnecessary weight.

Athlete Takeaways

- Clean baton exchanges require clear communication
- Teach money fundamentals early and consistently
- Coach young adults without running their race
- Plan for aging parents before crisis hits
- Boundaries protect relationships and performance

Part VI: Finishing Strong

Every runner knows the final phase of a race is not about talent alone. It is about discipline, awareness, and execution when fatigue sets in. Form matters more. Decisions matter more. Small mistakes that were manageable earlier become costly near the finish.

Money works the same way.

Finishing strong financially is not about one big move late in life. It is about avoiding unforced errors, protecting what you have built, and staying patient when distractions are loud. This part of the book focuses on long-term judgment. Who you trust. What you avoid. How you stay focused when shortcuts, scams, and bad advice show up.

This is where experience matters. It is where perspective matters. It is where many people stumble, not because they lack intelligence, but because they stop respecting the basics.

In this final section, the goal is simple.

Stay disciplined.

Protect your progress.

Finish the race with control and confidence.

Strong seasons end well because the fundamentals never disappear.

Chapter 25: Advisors, Scams, and Long-Term Success

Every track athlete knows the last phase of a race is the most dangerous.

Your legs are heavy. Your breathing is loud. Your mind starts negotiating. This is where people tighten up, panic, or abandon the plan they trained for. The athletes who finish strong are not the ones who suddenly become faster. They are the ones who stay composed, trust their preparation, and avoid mistakes when fatigue sets in.

Money works the same way.

Long-term financial success is rarely destroyed by one dramatic decision. It is usually undone by poor guidance, bad information, or shortcuts taken late in the race. This chapter is about judgment. Who you listen to. Who you trust. What you ignore. And how you protect the progress you have already made.

When to Seek Professional Help

Track athletes use coaches for a reason.

You may know how to run, but a coach sees form breakdowns you miss. They understand training cycles, recovery, and race strategy from a higher vantage point. Getting help is not weakness. It is efficiency.

Financial professionals serve the same role.

You should consider professional help when:

- Your finances become more complex than your time or knowledge allows
- You experience a major life change such as a career shift, marriage, divorce, inheritance, or business opportunity
- You start earning more money than you have ever managed before
- You feel overwhelmed or paralyzed by decisions
- You want a second set of eyes to pressure-test your plan

In track terms, this is moving from training alone to structured coaching. You can still run your race, but guidance helps you avoid preventable mistakes.

The key is not just *getting* help. It is getting the *right* help.

Types of Financial Advisors

Not all advisors play the same role. This is where many athletes get confused.

In track terms, you would never confuse a sprint coach, distance coach, and strength coach. Each has a different focus. Financial advisors are similar.

Common types include:

Commission-Based Advisors

They earn money by selling products. Insurance and investment commissions are common here. Some are knowledgeable. Others are sales-driven.

Track analogy: A shoe rep pushing one brand regardless of fit.

Fee-Based or Fee-Only Advisors

They are paid directly by clients through flat fees, hourly fees, or a percentage of assets managed. Their incentives are usually more aligned with long-term planning.

Track analogy: A coach paid to develop you over seasons, not just sell you equipment.

Registered Investment Advisors (RIAs)

These advisors operate under a fiduciary standard, meaning they are legally required to act in your best interest.

Track analogy: A coach accountable for your health, performance, and longevity.

Specialists

Tax professionals, estate attorneys, insurance specialists. These are not generalists. They handle specific parts of the race.

Track analogy: Physical therapists, nutritionists, and strength coaches.

One advisor does not have to do everything. In fact, good advisors know when to bring in others.

Recognizing Scams and Bad Advice

Scams target athletes for one reason.

Opportunity.

Athletes often have income spikes, visibility, and confidence. Scammers know this. They also know athletes are used to trusting authority figures and teammates.

Common red flags include:

- Guaranteed returns
- Pressure to act quickly
- "Everyone is doing this"
- Complex explanations that cannot be simplified
- Promises of exclusivity
- Dismissal of risk
- Avoidance of written documentation

In track terms, this is someone promising a shortcut to peak performance with no training, no recovery, and no downside. You already know that does not exist.

Bad advice is not always malicious. Sometimes it is just wrong.

Bad advice often sounds like:

- "You're young, take as much risk as possible"
- "Debt doesn't matter if payments are small"

- "This worked for me, so it will work for you"
- "Markets always go up"
- "You can fix this later"

Track teaches context. Event, distance, body type, and training age all matter. Money is no different. What works for one person can break another.

Ten Common Financial Mistakes Athletes Make

1. **Confusing income with wealth**
2. Fast times feel good. So do big paychecks. Neither guarantee longevity.
3. **Skipping the base**
4. No savings. No emergency fund. Straight to risk.
5. **Taking advice from the loudest voice**
6. Confidence is not competence.
7. **Chasing trends and hype**
8. Fast times fade. Discipline lasts.
9. **Using debt to fund lifestyle**
10. That is running with a weighted vest.
11. **Ignoring taxes until it hurts**
12. That is racing without knowing the course.
13. **Avoiding paperwork and details**
14. Missed details cost championships.
15. **Delaying hard decisions**
16. Fatigue makes problems worse, not better.
17. **Overestimating future income**
18. You train for today, not assumptions.
19. **Waiting too long to ask for help**
20. Injuries ignored early become season-ending.

Ten Rules for Long-Term Success

These are not hacks. They are fundamentals.

1. **Respect the base**
2. Cash flow, savings, protection first.
3. **Pace yourself**
4. You do not sprint the first lap of a long race.
5. **Protect flexibility**
6. Options keep you calm under pressure.
7. **Demand clarity**
8. If you cannot explain it, do not invest in it.
9. **Avoid shortcuts**
10. They always cost more later.
11. **Separate ego from decisions**
12. Money does not care who you used to be.
13. **Automate discipline**
14. Systems beat motivation.
15. **Review the plan regularly**
16. Adjust without panic.
17. **Choose advisors like coaches**
18. Alignment matters more than charisma.
19. **Finish strong**
20. Long-term success is about endurance, not flash.

Coach's Perspective

A track coach would not sugarcoat this.

Stay in your lane.

Trust the plan.

Do not chase the pack.

Control what you can control.

Finish the race you trained for.

Nobody wins because they panicked at the bell lap. Winners win because they prepared for fatigue.

Game Situations and Decision Points

You are offered an "exclusive" investment.

Do you evaluate it calmly, or fear missing out?

You meet an advisor who talks fast and promises certainty.

Do you slow the conversation or get swept up?

You feel financially behind compared to peers.

Do you force moves, or trust your pace?

Every race has these moments.

Common Athlete Mistakes and Financial Parallels

Athletes panic when the pack surges.

Financially, that looks like chasing trends.

Athletes ignore form late in races.

Financially, that looks like sloppy decisions.

Athletes trust adrenaline over preparation.

Financially, that looks like emotional investing.

Winning the Long Game

Track careers end. Financial lives do not.

The goal is not to be perfect. The goal is to stay healthy, disciplined, and consistent long enough to finish strong. Athletes who succeed after competition are not the ones who ran the fastest early. They are the ones who respected pacing, sought good coaching, avoided distractions, and stayed focused when it mattered most.

Athlete Takeaways

- Choose advisors like coaches, not hype men
- If it sounds like a shortcut, it probably is
- Discipline beats urgency late in the race
- Protect what you've built before chasing more
- Finish strong by staying in your lane

Chapter 26: Losing the Schedule and Rebuilding Structure

Every track athlete remembers the schedule.

Morning lifts. Afternoon practice. Assigned mileage. Recovery windows. Travel itineraries. Meet days planned weeks in advance. Someone else decided when you trained, when you rested, and when you competed. You did not have to negotiate with yourself. You just showed up and executed.

Then one day, the schedule disappears.

No practice time on the calendar. No coach checking attendance. No training plan taped to the locker. No meet circled in red ink. The structure that quietly held everything together is gone, and suddenly life feels heavier than it ever did during competition.

This is one of the most overlooked transitions athletes face, and it has a direct impact on money.

Why Life Gets Harder When No One Is Setting Your Calendar

Track is a sport built on structure. You do not train randomly. You follow cycles. Base phases. Speed phases. Tapering. Recovery. Everything has a purpose tied to timing.

When that structure vanishes, most athletes assume freedom will make life easier. Instead, the opposite happens.

Without a schedule:

- Decisions multiply
- Discipline becomes optional
- Small delays turn into long-term drift

In track terms, this is like showing up to a season with no training plan and telling yourself you will "run when you feel like it." You might stay fit for a while, but progress stalls. Injuries increase. Performance drops quietly, not all at once.

Financial habits work the same way.

When no one sets your calendar, money decisions shift from planned to reactive. Bills get paid late. Saving becomes inconsistent. Investing gets postponed. Nothing feels urgent until something breaks.

From Mandatory Workouts to Optional Discipline

Mandatory workouts remove negotiation.

You did not debate whether to train. You trained because it was part of the system. Discipline was external at first, then internal over time.

After sports, everything becomes optional.

You can skip budgeting.

You can delay saving.

You can ignore account balances.

You can push decisions to "next month."

In track terms, this is like skipping easy mileage because it does not feel important. You do not feel the cost immediately. But weeks later, fitness is gone and race day exposes it.

Financial discipline works the same way. Missing one savings transfer does not hurt. Ignoring one statement does not feel dangerous. Over time, those skipped reps compound into instability.

The hardest part is not learning what to do. It is learning to do it without external enforcement.

How Lack of Structure Quietly Breaks Financial Habits

Most financial breakdowns are not dramatic. They are gradual.

Structure disappears.

Habits loosen.

Decisions get delayed.

Stress increases.

Mistakes follow.

Without a system:

- Money gets spent before it is assigned
- Saving happens only when convenient
- Long-term goals get replaced by short-term relief

In track terms, this is poor pacing. You go out too fast early, feel fine for a lap or two, then fade badly when it matters.

Athletes often blame income when things feel tight. In reality, the issue is often the absence of structure, not lack of ability.

You are trained to follow plans. When the plan disappears, confusion replaces confidence.

Replacing Practice Schedules With Personal Systems

The solution is not motivation. It is structure.

Great post-career athletes rebuild systems that mirror training environments, even if they do not look the same.

You need:

- A money schedule
- Automatic systems
- Regular check-ins
- Defined routines

In track terms, this is creating your own training plan after college. No coach writes it for you, but you still train with intention.

Financial structure can look like:

- Automatic savings on payday
- Bills scheduled, not remembered
- Monthly financial check-ins
- Annual goal reviews

These systems remove decision fatigue. They protect you from emotional choices. They allow progress even when life gets busy.

Why Self-Imposed Structure Is Harder But Stronger

External structure is powerful. Internal structure is permanent.

When you design your own systems, you stop relying on pressure and start relying on process. This is the difference between racing because a coach is watching and racing because you respect the work.

Financial success after sports requires the same shift.

You are no longer preparing for one meet. You are preparing for decades. That demands sustainable habits, not short bursts of effort.

In track terms, this is training for the long season, not just opening day.

Coach's Perspective

If a coach were addressing this transition, the message would be blunt.

Do not wait for someone else to hold you accountable.

Train like a pro.

Structure wins races.

Discipline beats motivation.

If you want consistency, build systems.

Coaches know that talent without structure wastes potential. The same is true with money.

Game Situations and Decision Points

You no longer have a set payday routine.

Do you let money drift, or do you assign it immediately?

Your calendar is wide open.

Do you schedule financial check-ins, or let months pass unnoticed?

Life feels busy and unstructured.

Do you delay decisions, or rebuild routines that create stability?

These are not dramatic choices. They are daily ones. Over time, they determine outcomes.

Common Athlete Mistakes and Financial Parallels

Athletes rely on pressure to perform.

Financially, that leads to procrastination without deadlines.

Athletes skip base work once competition ends.

Financially, that leads to broken habits.

Athletes mistake freedom for progress.

Financially, that leads to drift.

The discipline that built your career still matters. It just has to be self-directed now.

Winning the Long Game

Track teaches patience, pacing, and respect for the process. Those lessons do not expire when competition ends.

Losing the schedule is not failure. It is a transition.

Rebuilding structure is how you stay sharp, protect momentum, and avoid financial burnout. The athletes who succeed long-term are not the most aggressive. They are the most consistent.

They rebuild routines.

They schedule discipline.

They trust systems over emotion.

That is how you keep moving forward when no one is watching.

Athlete Takeaways

- Structure beats motivation when the season never ends
- Missing small reps quietly breaks momentum
- Self-imposed systems replace lost schedules
- Discipline is pacing, not punishment
- Build routines that carry you long after the finish line

Chapter 27: From Teammates to Coworkers

Every track athlete knows exactly who is on their team.

You know who you warm up with. You know who pushes the pace in workouts. You know who leads drills and who needs encouragement late in reps. Roles are clear, expectations are explicit, and feedback is constant. If something goes wrong, you hear about it immediately. If something goes right, it shows up in times, places, and points.

Then you leave sport.

Suddenly, you are surrounded by coworkers, not teammates. The environment looks similar on the surface, but the rules underneath are completely different. And for many former athletes, this transition is more disorienting than they expect. It does not just affect identity or motivation. It directly impacts income growth, career stability, and long-term financial outcomes.

Why the Workplace Feels Foreign After Sports

Track and field is honest.

The stopwatch does not care who you like.

The results do not care about office politics.

Performance is visible.

The workplace is different.

Success is often indirect. Progress is harder to measure. Expectations are rarely written out. Feedback is inconsistent. Advancement depends on more than effort alone.

For athletes used to clear systems, this feels uncomfortable. You are no longer judged by splits or finishes. You are judged by perceptions, communication, and alignment with goals that are not always explained.

In track terms, this is like showing up to a race without knowing the distance, the scoring system, or how qualification works. You might still compete hard, but confusion costs you efficiency.

Authority Without Coaches

In sport, authority is obvious.

The coach sets the plan.

The coach evaluates performance.

The coach decides who runs.

In the workplace, authority is often indirect.

Managers may not have coached before.

Leaders may not give technical feedback.

Decision-makers may not observe your daily effort.

This creates a gap former athletes struggle with. You are used to being coached. You want instruction, correction, and clarity. Instead, you get autonomy without guidance.

In track terms, this is like being handed a training schedule with no explanation and being told to figure it out on your own. Some athletes thrive. Others overtrain, undertrain, or miss the point entirely.

Financially, this matters because unclear authority leads to missed opportunities. Raises are not automatic. Promotions are not guaranteed. Waiting to be noticed can stall income growth for years.

Feedback Without Film

Athletes live on feedback.

Film sessions.

Split times.

Race results.

Immediate correction.

In most workplaces, feedback is delayed, vague, or nonexistent. You may not know you are off course until review season. You may not know you are excelling until someone leaves and your workload increases.

This lack of feedback creates anxiety and overthinking. Former athletes often replay conversations the way they once replayed races, searching for meaning that may not be there.

In track terms, this is racing without splits. You are running hard, but you have no idea if the pace is right.

Financially, poor feedback loops lead to stagnation. Without clarity, athletes may undersell themselves, avoid negotiation, or stay too long in roles that no longer serve them.

Politics, Ambiguity, and Unclear Expectations

Track is merit-based, even when it hurts.

The workplace is not always.

Relationships matter.

Visibility matters.

Timing matters.

This feels unfair to athletes trained to believe effort equals outcome. When that equation breaks, frustration sets in. Some athletes disengage. Others overwork. Both responses can hurt long-term stability.

In track terms, this is like racing in a tactical event where positioning matters as much as fitness. If you ignore strategy, you get boxed in, no matter how strong you are.

Understanding workplace dynamics is not selling out. It is learning the race conditions. Athletes who adapt build resilience. Those who refuse struggle longer than necessary.

How This Impacts Income Growth and Career Stability

Careers are the longest events you will ever run.

Income growth depends on:

- Skill development
- Communication
- Timing
- Visibility
- Negotiation

Athletes who wait for clear lanes often get passed. Athletes who learn the system position themselves better.

Without adaptation:

- Raises lag behind inflation
- Job changes happen reactively
- Financial planning becomes unstable

In track terms, this is running without pacing awareness. You may finish, but not where you should have.

Career instability leads to financial stress. Financial stress leads to poor decisions. The cycle feeds itself unless interrupted intentionally.

Learning to Translate Athletic Skills Into Workplace Value

Athletes have transferable skills, but they are not always recognized automatically.

Discipline.

Consistency.

Coachability.

Resilience.

Preparation.

The mistake is assuming others see these qualities without explanation.

In track terms, this is assuming everyone understands your training background without seeing your race results. You still have to show it.

Learning to communicate value is part of professional maturity. This includes:

- Asking for feedback directly
- Clarifying expectations
- Advocating for growth
- Negotiating compensation

These are not selfish acts. They are professional ones.

Coach's Perspective

If a coach were preparing you for this transition, the message would be familiar.

Know the rules of the race.

Do not wait to be told.

Control what you can control.

Adapt to conditions.

Compete where you are.

The workplace is not unfair. It is just different. Winning requires understanding the environment.

Game Situations and Decision Points

You are working hard but feel invisible.

Do you wait to be noticed, or ask for clarity?

You are unsure how performance is measured.

Do you guess, or seek feedback?

You feel underpaid for your role.

Do you complain quietly, or prepare for a professional conversation?

These moments determine income trajectory more than talent alone.

Common Athlete Mistakes and Financial Parallels

Athletes expect clear lanes.

Financially, that leads to missed advancement.

Athletes rely on effort alone.

Financially, that leads to stagnant pay.

Athletes avoid uncomfortable conversations.

Financially, that delays growth.

The same adaptability that wins races wins careers.

Winning the Long Game

The transition from teammates to coworkers is not a loss. It is an evolution.

You are still competing. The rules are just different.

Athletes who learn the workplace race with awareness build stable careers, growing income, and long-term financial security. Those who refuse to adjust stay frustrated and underpaid longer than necessary.

You do not need to abandon who you are. You need to translate it.

Athlete Takeaways

- The workplace has different rules than sport
- Feedback is indirect, so you must seek it
- Effort matters, but positioning matters too
- Career growth drives financial stability
- Learn the race conditions and run smart

Chapter 28: When No One Is Watching Anymore

Every track athlete knows what it feels like to be watched.

Coaches line the track with clipboards. Teammates glance at splits. Someone is always counting reps, checking form, or calling out pace. Even when you are exhausted, the presence of eyes keeps you moving. Accountability is built into the environment.

Then sport ends.

No one checks if you woke up early.

No one tracks your reps.

No one notices if you cut a workout short.

No one calls you out if you skip preparation.

At first, the freedom feels great. Eventually, it becomes dangerous.

This is where many former athletes quietly struggle, not because they lack discipline, but because the structure that once enforced discipline is gone. And when accountability disappears, habits change. Those habit changes show up years later, often in the form of money mistakes.

The Discipline Gap After Accountability Disappears

Track is a controlled environment.

Training plans are written.

Competitions are scheduled.

Consequences are immediate.

Adult life is not.

Deadlines are flexible.

Standards are implied.

Consequences are delayed.

That delay is the problem.

When consequences do not show up immediately, discipline weakens. Skipping one workout rarely matters. Skipping one savings contribution feels harmless. Missing one budget check-in feels insignificant.

But repetition works both ways.

In track terms, this is drifting off pace early in a long race. You may not feel it at the first lap, but it shows up late when you are empty and wondering where the strength went.

Financial discipline erodes quietly. There is no whistle. No penalty flag. Just slow drift.

Why Former Athletes Self-Sabotage Without Pressure

Athletes are trained to respond to pressure.

Deadlines.

Competition.

Expectation.

Remove those, and many athletes lose urgency. Not because they are lazy, but because they were conditioned to perform when stakes were visible.

Money stakes are invisible at first.

Overspending does not hurt immediately.

Skipping savings does not feel painful.

Ignoring debt still allows you to live comfortably.

Until it does not.

Former athletes often say, "I'll fix it later." Later becomes years. The damage compounds silently.

In track terms, this is ignoring small form breakdowns. You can get away with it for a while. Eventually, injury shows up.

Self-sabotage is rarely intentional. It is usually the absence of pressure combined with the assumption that discipline will return when needed. It rarely does without structure.

Comfort vs Growth Decisions

Track teaches discomfort.

Intervals hurt.

Training blocks are exhausting.

Progress requires strain.

Adult life rewards comfort.

Convenience.

Entertainment.

Lifestyle upgrades.

The danger is subtle. Comfort decisions feel earned. Growth decisions feel optional.

Financially, comfort looks like:

- Lifestyle inflation
- Convenience spending
- Avoiding hard conversations
- Delaying planning

Growth looks like:

- Saving before spending
- Investing consistently
- Saying no to upgrades
- Staying uncomfortable longer

In track terms, this is choosing between cruising and pressing. One maintains, the other improves.

Former athletes often choose comfort because no one is watching anymore. There is no coach demanding more. But growth still requires discomfort, even when the crowd is gone.

Translating "Grind Culture" Into Adult Life

Athletes know how to grind.

Early mornings.

Late nights.

Repetitive work.

The mistake is assuming grind alone creates results.

In adult life, grinding without direction leads to burnout. Grinding without systems leads to wasted effort. Grinding without feedback leads to frustration.

Financial discipline is not about grinding harder. It is about grinding smarter.

Automatic savings.

Scheduled reviews.

Clear goals.

Simple systems.

In track terms, this is efficient training. You do not run max effort every day. You follow a plan.

Former athletes often overwork and underplan. That imbalance shows up in money as reactive decisions instead of intentional ones.

Why Money Mistakes Show Up Years Later

Money mistakes are delayed penalties.

Skipping savings at 25 shows up at 40.

Ignoring retirement early shows up late.

Lifestyle creep compounds quietly.

This delay makes money dangerous for athletes. In sport, mistakes are immediate. In finance, mistakes are invisible until they are not.

In track terms, this is poor base training. You can race well for a season. Eventually, performance drops and you do not know why.

Most financial regret is not about bad investments. It is about lack of structure during years when discipline should have been easiest.

Rebuilding Accountability Without External Pressure

The solution is not more motivation.

Motivation fades.

Systems remain.

Former athletes need to replace external accountability with internal systems.

This includes:

- Automating good decisions
- Scheduling financial check-ins
- Setting clear goals with timelines
- Creating consequences for inaction

In track terms, this is training solo but still following the plan.

You are responsible now. That is not a loss. It is maturity.

Coach's Perspective

If a coach were still watching, the message would be blunt.

Nobody is coming to save you.

Comfort is the enemy.

Discipline is a choice now.

You are responsible for the outcome.

The absence of a whistle does not mean the race ended. It means you are leading yourself.

Game Situations and Decision Points

You get a raise.

Do you upgrade your lifestyle, or upgrade your future?

No one checks your savings rate.

Do you ignore it, or build a system anyway?

You feel comfortable financially.

Do you coast, or keep training?

These are late-race decisions. They define the finish.

Common Athlete Mistakes and Financial Parallels

Athletes rely on pressure.

Financially, that leads to drift.

Athletes chase comfort after sacrifice.

Financially, that leads to stagnation.

Athletes assume discipline is permanent.

Financially, that leads to neglect.

Awareness interrupts the cycle.

Winning the Long Game

Discipline is hardest when no one is watching.

That is also when it matters most.

Former athletes who rebuild structure win financially not because they are smarter, but because they respect the process. They treat money like training. Boring. Repetitive. Effective.

You do not need hype.

You do not need pressure.

You need systems.

The race did not end when the uniform came off. It just changed distance.

Athlete Takeaways

- Discipline fades without structure, not effort
- Comfort decisions quietly limit growth
- Grind needs systems to work long-term
- Money mistakes are delayed penalties
- Lead yourself like a pro and finish strong

Chapter 29: Redefining Winning After the Uniform Comes Off

Every track athlete remembers the scoreboard.

Times.

Placings.

Qualifying marks.

Personal records.

Winning was clear. You either hit the standard or you did not. You either advanced or you went home. The rules were defined, and the scoreboard never lied.

Then the uniform comes off.

There is no official scoreboard anymore.

No rankings.

No heats.

No finish tape.

And without realizing it, many former athletes start chasing the wrong markers of success.

Why Chasing Status Replaces Chasing Performance

In track, performance is everything.

You cannot fake a time.

You cannot talk your way into a PR.

You cannot buy your way onto the podium.

After sports, performance becomes harder to measure. Progress feels abstract. Growth is slower. Feedback is inconsistent. Into that vacuum steps status.

Income.

Job titles.

Houses.

Cars.

Social media signals.

Status is visible. Performance is not.

Former athletes often shift from chasing performance to chasing proof. Proof that they are still winning. Proof that they are still progressing. Proof that the sacrifice meant something.

The problem is that status is a poor substitute for performance.

In track terms, this is caring more about the warm-up gear than the race result. It looks good, but it does not move the clock.

Income vs Fulfillment

Money is a score, but it is not the whole scoreboard.

Income measures what you earn.

Fulfillment measures how you live.

Many former athletes chase income alone because it is the easiest number to track. Bigger paycheck equals winning. Smaller paycheck equals falling behind.

But income without fulfillment feels hollow. Fulfillment without income feels stressful. The balance matters.

In track terms, this is pacing.

You cannot sprint the entire race.

You cannot jog if the event demands speed.

Winning requires alignment between effort, ability, and distance.

Financially, that alignment looks like:

- Earning enough to support your life

- Spending in ways that reflect your values
- Building long-term security
- Maintaining flexibility and health

Chasing income alone often leads to burnout. Chasing fulfillment without structure often leads to instability. Winning requires both.

Titles, Houses, Cars, and Comparison Traps

Track teaches comparison early.

You know who is faster.

You know who qualified.

You know where you stand.

After sports, comparison becomes distorted.

You compare highlight reels.

You compare milestones without context.

You compare outcomes without seeing the training cycle.

Titles sound impressive.

Houses look permanent.

Cars feel like arrival.

But none of those guarantee stability, happiness, or progress.

In track terms, this is comparing splits without knowing the event. A fast 200 does not mean much in a 5K. Context matters.

Former athletes fall into comparison traps because competition is wired into them. The danger is competing in events they never chose.

Buying things to prove success often delays actual success.

The Hidden Cost of Chasing Status

Status is expensive.

Not just financially, but emotionally.

Lifestyle inflation.

Long-term debt.

Stress.

Pressure to maintain appearances.

Many former athletes look successful on the outside and feel trapped on the inside. They built a life that looks like winning but feels like obligation.

In track terms, this is running someone else's race plan. You may finish, but it is never clean.

Financial success is not about impressing others. It is about building a system that supports your life, not constrains it.

What "Success" Actually Looks Like in Your 30s and 40s

Real success changes shape over time.

In your 20s, success may look like opportunity and momentum.

In your 30s, it often looks like stability and flexibility.

In your 40s, it looks like control and choice.

For former athletes, success often means:

- Less financial stress
- More optionality
- Time with family
- Health and longevity
- Work that aligns with values
- Confidence about the future

These are not flashy metrics. They do not trend online. They matter more than any title ever did.

In track terms, this is finishing strong instead of burning out early.

Building a New Scoreboard

You need a new scoreboard.

Not one based on comparison.

Not one based on appearances.

One based on alignment and control.

A healthy financial scoreboard includes:

- Positive cash flow
- Growing net worth
- Manageable debt
- Consistent investing
- Emergency reserves
- Freedom to make choices

This scoreboard is quiet. It does not announce itself. It rewards discipline, not attention.

Former athletes who build this scoreboard stop feeling behind. They stop chasing. They start executing.

Letting Go of the Old Uniform

This is one of the hardest transitions.

The uniform represented identity.

The sport represented certainty.

The scoreboard represented worth.

Letting go does not mean forgetting. It means transferring lessons.

Discipline.

Preparation.

Delayed gratification.

Process over results.

Those skills still matter. They just apply differently now.

In track terms, this is moving from competition season to long-term training. The work changes. The purpose remains.

Coach's Perspective

If a coach were speaking honestly, it would sound familiar.

Stop worrying about what it looks like.

Run your race.

Control what you can control.

Compete with yourself.

Finish strong.

The loudest scoreboard is rarely the most important.

Game Situations and Decision Points

You get promoted.

Do you upgrade your lifestyle immediately, or strengthen your foundation first?

You see peers buying bigger homes.

Do you compare, or evaluate what fits your race?

You feel successful but stressed.

Do you ask why, or keep pushing?

These are mid-career decisions. They shape the back half of the race.

Common Athlete Mistakes and Financial Parallels

Athletes chase podiums.

Financially, that becomes status chasing.

Athletes compare splits.

Financially, that becomes lifestyle comparison.

Athletes ignore pacing.

Financially, that leads to burnout and regret.

Awareness changes direction.

Winning the Long Game

Winning after sports is not louder. It is quieter.

It looks like sleeping well.

It looks like options.

It looks like peace with your choices.

It looks like control instead of urgency.

Former athletes who redefine winning stop chasing validation and start building stability. They do not need to prove anything. They execute.

The finish line is not one moment. It is decades.

Athlete Takeaways

- Status is visible, performance is sustainable
- Income matters, but fulfillment determines pace
- Comparison traps derail long-term success
- Build a scoreboard based on control and freedom
- Run your race and finish strong

Chapter 30: Staying Connected Without Living in the Past

Every track athlete knows what it feels like to belong to a team, even in an individual sport.

You trained together.

You warmed up together.

You traveled together.

You suffered together.

Even when races were individual, the environment was collective. There was always a locker room, a training group, a coach, a schedule, and a shared sense of purpose. You knew where you fit. You knew who you were running with and why.

Then the season ends.

The uniform comes off.

And quietly, that structure disappears.

What many former athletes underestimate is not the loss of competition. It is the loss of connection.

The Role of Community, Mentorship, and New Locker Rooms

In track, progress does not happen alone.

Training groups matter.

Coaches matter.

Teammates matter.

Even the most disciplined athletes benefit from shared accountability. Showing up is easier when others expect you. Pushing is easier when someone else is grinding beside you.

After sports, that system is gone. No one assigns training partners. No one builds your schedule. No one checks attendance.

Financially and emotionally, this is where people drift.

Community provides:

- Perspective when you lose clarity
- Accountability when motivation dips
- Belonging when identity feels shaky

Mentorship provides:

- Guidance without judgment
- Experience you have not lived yet
- Shortcuts around preventable mistakes

New locker rooms provide:

- A place to belong
- A shared mission
- Forward momentum

Without replacing these intentionally, isolation fills the gap.

Why Isolation Hits Former Athletes Hard

Isolation does not always feel lonely at first.

It feels quiet.

It feels like freedom.

It feels like finally being in control.

But over time, isolation erodes discipline.

Former athletes are used to structure and shared struggle. When that disappears, the mind often fills the space with comparison, regret, or stagnation.

Isolation hits former athletes hard because:

- Identity was tied to the team
- Feedback was constant and immediate
- Belonging was built in

When those disappear, it can feel like losing your footing mid-race. You are still moving, but something feels off.

Financial mistakes often follow isolation. Not because of lack of intelligence, but because decisions are made without perspective or accountability.

Finding Purpose Without the Team

Purpose does not disappear when sports end.

But it does change shape.

In track, purpose was clear.

Train.

Compete.

Improve.

Advance.

After sports, purpose becomes self-directed. That is empowering, but also disorienting.

Former athletes often struggle here because they wait for purpose to be assigned instead of built.

Purpose after sports is often found through:

- Work that aligns with values
- Mentoring others
- Building something long-term
- Contributing beyond yourself

- Creating stability for family

This is not about replacing track.

It is about transferring meaning.

In track terms, this is moving from competition season to legacy building. The effort remains. The destination evolves.

Healthy Nostalgia vs Being Stuck

Nostalgia is natural.

Remembering races.

Laughing about training stories.

Feeling pride in what you accomplished.

Healthy nostalgia honors the past without living there.

Being stuck looks different.

- Constantly reliving peak moments
- Comparing everything to "back then"
- Feeling resentful that nothing matches it
- Using past identity as a shield against growth

In track terms, this is watching old race footage instead of training for the next event. It feels good, but it does not move you forward.

Healthy nostalgia says, "That mattered."

Being stuck says, "That was all that mattered."

The difference is intention.

Creating a Forward-Looking Identity

You are not the same person you were in your competitive years.

That is not loss.

That is growth.

A forward-looking identity integrates who you were with who you are becoming.

Former athletes who thrive do not erase their past. They repurpose it. They carry forward:

- Discipline
- Work ethic
- Resilience
- Coachability
- Competitive drive

They release:

- The need for constant validation
- Comparison-based worth
- Identity tied to performance alone

In track terms, this is adapting training as the season changes. The fundamentals stay. The application evolves.

Community as a Financial Advantage

This matters more than most people realize.

Isolation leads to:

- Poor financial decisions
- Emotional spending
- Short-term thinking
- Lack of accountability

Community provides:

- Shared learning
- Better decision-making

- Long-term thinking
- Normalization of patience

The strongest financial outcomes often come from people who are not doing it alone.

They ask questions.

They share experiences.

They learn from others' mistakes.

They stay grounded.

Coach's Perspective

A coach would not let this slide.

You don't do this alone.

Find your people.

Stay connected.

Be part of something bigger than yourself.

Don't disappear.

Isolation is not toughness. It is vulnerability without support.

Game Situations and Decision Points

You leave sports and focus only on work.

Do you replace community, or assume you do not need it?

You miss the team environment.

Do you chase the past, or build something new?

You feel disconnected.

Do you isolate further, or reach out?

These decisions shape the next chapter more than any financial move.

Common Athlete Mistakes and Financial Parallels

Athletes train alone too long.

Financially, that means making decisions in a vacuum.

Athletes chase old highs.

Financially, that means nostalgia-driven choices.

Athletes resist new roles.

Financially, that means stagnation.

Connection creates momentum.

Winning the Long Game

Life after sports is not about recreating the past.

It is about honoring it while moving forward.

Staying connected does not mean staying stuck.

It means finding new locker rooms.

New teammates.

New goals.

Former athletes who thrive build community intentionally. They seek mentorship. They contribute. They stay engaged with life, not just memories.

The race does not end when competition does.

It changes distance.

Finish it with people around you.

Athlete Takeaways

- Community replaces structure when sports end
- Isolation quietly erodes discipline and clarity
- Honor the past without living there
- Build a forward-looking identity rooted in fundamentals
- Find new locker rooms and keep moving forward

Glossary of Track and Financial Terms

This glossary connects key financial concepts to familiar ideas from **track and field**, making money easier to understand through the language, structure, and discipline athletes already know.

Asset Allocation

Financial Definition:

How money is divided among different investment types such as stocks, bonds, and cash to balance risk and return.

Track Comparison:

How effort is distributed across events, training phases, and energy systems. Too much focus on one phase without balance leads to burnout or poor race execution.

Assets

Financial Definition:

Things you own that have value, such as cash, investments, real estate, or retirement accounts.

Track Comparison:

Your athletic strengths. Speed, endurance, technique, experience, and preparation that contribute to overall performance.

Bonds

Financial Definition:

Loans made to governments or companies that pay interest and return principal over time.

Track Comparison:

Base mileage. Not flashy, but essential for stability, endurance, and control when races get long or conditions get tough.

Budget

Financial Definition:

A plan for how income is allocated toward expenses, savings, and goals.

Track Comparison:

Training splits or pacing charts. Without knowing the plan, execution breaks down early.

Cash Flow

Financial Definition:

Money coming in versus money going out.

Track Comparison:

Energy management. Go out too fast and you struggle to finish the race.

Compounding

Financial Definition:

Earnings that generate additional earnings over time.

Track Comparison:

Daily mileage and consistent workouts. Each session builds on the last and makes progress easier over time.

Credit

Financial Definition:

The ability to borrow money with the promise of repayment.

Track Comparison:

Trust with your coach. Earned through consistency, lost quickly through mistakes.

Debt

Financial Definition:

Money borrowed that must be repaid, often with interest.

Track Comparison:

Training with added weight. Manageable in small amounts, dangerous when excessive.

Diversification

Financial Definition:

Spreading investments across different assets to reduce risk.

Track Comparison:

Not relying on one event, one race, or one strength to define your entire season.

Emergency Fund

Financial Definition:

Savings set aside for unexpected expenses.

Track Comparison:

Injury reserves and recovery days. You hope you do not need them, but they keep you in the season.

ETF (Exchange-Traded Fund)

Financial Definition:

A fund that holds many investments and trades like a stock.

Track Comparison:

Team relays or training groups. Shared effort instead of solo risk.

Fees / Expense Ratios

Financial Definition:

Costs associated with managing investments.

Track Comparison:

Poor mechanics or wasted motion. Small inefficiencies that quietly slow you down over time.

Growth Investing

Financial Definition:

Investing in companies expected to grow faster than average.

Track Comparison:

High-intensity workouts. More upside, but only effective when fundamentals are solid.

Insurance

Financial Definition:

Protection against financial loss from unexpected events.

Track Comparison:

Medical staff and recovery protocols. You do not race without protection when risk is high.

Liquidity

Financial Definition:

How easily money can be accessed without penalty or delay.

Track Comparison:

Tactical flexibility. The ability to adjust pace when the race changes.

Net Worth

Financial Definition:

Assets minus liabilities.

Track Comparison:

Season results. Not one race, but the full body of work.

Rebalancing

Financial Definition:

Adjusting investments back to their intended mix over time.

Track Comparison:

Mid-season training adjustments to restore balance and prevent burnout.

Risk

Financial Definition:

The chance that outcomes differ from expectations, including loss.

Track Comparison:

Race strategy selection. Higher reward often comes with higher risk.

Roth IRA

Financial Definition:

A retirement account where money grows tax-free if rules are followed.

Track Comparison:

Front-loading training work so the finish is smoother and stronger later.

Stocks

Financial Definition:

Ownership shares in a company.

Track Comparison:

Primary race efforts. They drive progress but require support and discipline.

Tax-Advantaged Accounts

Financial Definition:

Accounts that provide tax benefits, often with rules and restrictions.

Track Comparison:

Structured training cycles. Rules exist to improve long-term outcomes.

Volatility

Financial Definition:

Short-term ups and downs in market value.

Track Comparison:

Pace fluctuations during a race. Normal unless you panic and abandon form.

Permanent Loss

Financial Definition:

Money that cannot recover due to poor decisions or panic.

Track Comparison:

A pulled muscle from ignoring fundamentals. Usually avoidable.

Total Return

Financial Definition:

Investment return from both price growth and income.

Track Comparison:

Overall race result. Every lap matters, not just the finish kick.

Value Investing

Financial Definition:

Investing in assets believed to be undervalued.

Track Comparison:

Efficient pacing. Less flash, more control, consistent results.

Yield

Financial Definition:

Income generated from an investment.

Track Comparison:

Steady scoring pace. Not dramatic, but reliable over distance.

Final Note

This glossary reinforces one core principle:

Financial success, like success in **track and field**, comes from balance, discipline, timing, and repetition.

That philosophy runs through **Track Money 101** and continues long after competition ends.

Disclaimers

This book is for **educational purposes only**.

The information provided in **Track Money 101** is intended to help readers understand general financial concepts using **track and field–based analogies**. It is not individualized financial, investment, tax, legal, or insurance advice.

Every financial situation is different. Your goals, income, family circumstances, risk tolerance, and time horizon are unique. What works for one athlete may not be appropriate for another.

Not Financial, Investment, or Legal Advice

Nothing in this book should be interpreted as a recommendation to buy, sell, or hold any specific investment, financial product, or strategy.

This book does not replace advice from qualified professionals such as:

- Financial advisors
- Accountants or tax professionals
- Attorneys
- Insurance professionals

Before making financial decisions, readers should consult professionals who can evaluate their individual situation.

No Guarantees or Promises of Results

All investing involves risk, including the possible loss of principal.

Past performance does not guarantee future results. Markets fluctuate. Economic conditions change. Outcomes cannot be predicted or guaranteed.

The examples and scenarios in this book are illustrative only and may not reflect actual results or real-world outcomes.

Tax and Legal Information

Any discussion of taxes, retirement accounts, estate planning, or legal structures is general in nature.

Tax laws and regulations change frequently and vary by jurisdiction. Legal requirements differ based on location and personal circumstances.

Readers should seek personalized tax or legal advice before acting on any information related to these topics.

Athlete and Career Considerations

This book discusses financial topics as they relate to athletes and former athletes, including career transitions and income changes.

It does not provide career placement services, employment advice, or guarantees related to income, compensation, or career success.

Use of Analogies

Track and field and sports analogies are used to make financial concepts easier to understand.

These analogies are educational tools only and should not be interpreted literally. Financial decisions require analysis beyond analogy.

Personal Responsibility

By reading this book, you acknowledge that:

- You are responsible for your own financial decisions
- You understand that financial outcomes involve uncertainty
- You agree to seek appropriate professional guidance when needed

Education improves decision-making, but responsibility remains with the individual.

Contact Information

If you would like to learn more about the concepts discussed in this book or explore additional educational resources, **Pat Brown** can be found through public platforms including LinkedIn, Twitter, and via Google search.

For questions specifically related to **Track Money 101**, you may contact Pat Brown at:

info@trackmoney101.com *(replace if using a different book-specific email)*

Final Reminder

Financial success is built over time through discipline, planning, and consistency.

This book provides a framework, not a guarantee.

Use it as a guide, not a substitute for professional advice.

Pat Brown OLB, University of Kansas

Made in the USA
Monee, IL
04 November 2026

67387611R00144